LLANGWYFAN MAGIC – VOLUME 2

"MEMORIES"

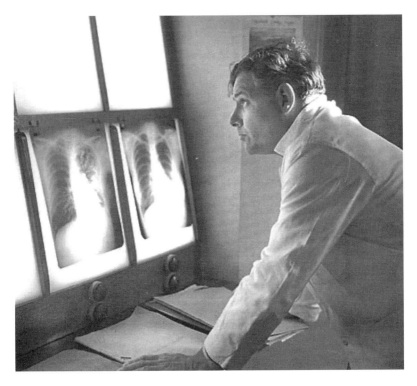

Dr R W Biagi, MBE, FRCP[Ed.]
1914-1990
Medical Superintendent – Llangwyfan 1951-1980

LLANGWYFAN MAGIC – VOLUME 2

"MEMORIES"

BUDDUG OWEN

ISBN 9-781904845-90-4

Printed by Gwasg y Bwthyn, Caernarfon

CONTENTS

DEDICATED TO

RICHARD, WILLIAM

AND

DAVID, GILLIAN

FOREWORD

Dr Buddug Owen's latest book is her third volume devoted to the story of the lives of patients, staff, benefactors and administrators of the Llangwyfan Sanatorium from its opening during World War I until it closed 60 years later. Nearly all TB sanatoria built at that time were isolated because of the risk of passing on an infectious disease that, for many years, was difficult to treat other than by general supportive therapy and rest. The King Edward VII Welsh National Memorial Association was set up to provide sanatorium care for TB patients in Wales. Talgarth, near Brecon and Llangwyfan, near Denbigh, were located in isolated rural areas in South and North Wales respectively. One story about these locations suggested that each catered for the TB population of the opposite part of Wales to discourage visiting by relatives and increase the reality of isolation and reduce the risk of contact with non infected relatives. In this volume Peter Wilson, who has one of the longest personal associations with both sanatoria, as both patient and member of staff, describes his experiences in both. For many years the mainstays of treatment were rest and fresh air. This meant that in winter the harsh conditions for nurses and patients resembled the Soviet gulag. But being confined to bed for many weeks, sometimes in freezing conditions, was not the worst treatment. One of the most remarkable accounts in this volume describes the mediaeval torture, as recently as the 1950s, of being held in whole body plaster cast for months on end and being unable to turn to one side by even a few degrees. Just to read about this was as horrific an experience as Edgar Alan Poe's story of "Premature Burial" and it is not surprising that the patient concerned has preferred to remain anonymous. The gradual evolution of experiences described in these pages speak for themselves; many examples illustrate the life-long culture of hard work, kindness, courtesy and inventiveness shared by all those who have contributed to this book. As the scientific treatment of TB developed so did the expertise in measuring the effect of TB and other diseases on the physiology of the lung. The ingenuity and determination of Mr Brian Cowlishaw in setting up such a superb lab is well described in this volume. In her three books on Llangwyfan Dr Owen also describes many of the world-class doctors and surgeons who provided a unique service to the patients at Llangwyfan. One surgeon, still operating at the Sanatorium into his mid 70s, was told that his operating days were over and his hair immediately turned white. Once again, Dr Owen's tenacity, powers of persuasion, and devotion to colleagues and patients have resulted in another extraordinarily valuable record of the many people who spent years of their lives at Llangwyfan. While TB itself has not gone away the isolated, self-sufficient, TB sanatorium having a staff with very close and long lasting personal ties, has disappeared, and this volume, like the two that came before, provides a rich vein of priceless pictures, anecdotes and characters from an age that has now all but vanished.

Prof J. Gareth Jones, University of Cambridge.

INTRODUCTION AND
ACKNOWLEDGEMENTS

Following the publication of "Llangwyfan – Sanatorium to Hospital" in 2007, I continued to collect material on the Institution, its connections, staff and patients and talked to anyone who was prepared to talk to me and give me their recollections. This has resulted a year later in enough material to offer to those who are interested a further insight into Llangwyfan and to share with the reader what my research has uncovered. I decided, on advice, to offer this work in two volumes. The first "Llangwyfan Magic – Lest we Forget" published in the Autumn 2008, and the second volume "Llangwyfan Magic – Memories" in the Spring 2009.

I have re-kindled old friendships and made new friends, and the continued journey has given me a great deal of pleasure. I have been able to correct some statements made in the first book and I would particularly like to point out that the Royal Opening took place on Friday, 16th July 1920. I have tried to fill gaps in knowledge, some of which have been difficult to ascertain, some people have been elusive whilst others have been very generous with oral and written testimony. My debt to them all has been enormous and I am grateful to the following for the help they have given me for both volumes:

June Arnold
Jane Baker
Tim Baker
Pat Barry

Ian Bellingham
Rachel Billings
Ron and Eleanor Blundell
Jane Brunning

D Buckley
Maelorwen Cerny
Sue Copp
June Cooper
Brian Cowlishaw
Eddie Davies
H Davies
Owen Daniel
Pam Davies
Elizabeth Edwards
Ellen Emslie
Betty Evans
Rhian Evans
Peter and David Gillow
Michael Griffith
Jean Green
Ted Groom
Barry Hamilton
Ken Hardy
Mary Hawkins
Desmond Healy
Clwyd Hughes
Gwilym Hughes
John Gwyn Hughes
Lewis Hunt
Rhys Huws
O M Jonathan
Anwen Jones
Bill and Haf Lewis Jones
Gladys Jones
Idris Jones
Iorwerth Lloyd Jones
Professor J Gareth Jones
Stanley Wyn Jones
Dr Mary Lewis, Vancouver

Joan Gwenllian Lloyd
   (née Hughes)
Edward Lyons
Rose McMahon
Kevin Mathias
Jean Moffat
Nia Morris
Lorraine Orger
Elwyn Owen
R M Owen
Nest Price
Edgar Rees
Jean Richards
Anne Roberts
Dewi Roberts
Doris Roberts
Emyr Frances Roberts
Pauline Roberts
Ann Roche
Robert Rouse
David Rowlands
Mossie and Mary Royles
Emma Scott
Eryl Smith
Alan Stringfellow
Anne Sutherland
Gwyn and Mari Thomas
Harry and Carrie Thompson
Margaret Todd
Maggie Watkins
Norma Wayne
Peter and Winnie Wilson
Iona Williams
Gwyn Pierce-Williams
Paul Williams

Some need special mention:

Dr K Mathias and his staff of the Archives Department, Denbighshire County Council in Ruthin, and in particular Jane Brunning, have helped me an enormous amount as has Sue Copp of the Flintshire Record Office in Hawarden, Eryl Smith, the Head Librarian of Glan Clwyd Hospital and Nia Morris and Jane Baker of the Library at Maelor Hospital, Wrexham.

Lorraine Orger has been an indispensable ally in typing the manuscript as has Maelorwen Cerny; Barry Hamilton with photography; Peter and Winnie Wilson with networking and Iona Williams with proof-reading. I would like to thank Professor J Gareth Jones of Leeds for writing the Foreword and also for his continuing interest, support and suggestions.

I have collected many photographs and thank all those who have so generously allowed me access to them and permission to publish them. I have been able to put some names on photographs which appeared in Llangwyfan Sanatorium to Hospital and include these as a record.

I am grateful for permission to publish photographs of Llangwyfan Hospital from the John Charles collection 1955, from the National Library of Wales. Also photographs from Denbighshire Record Office and Flintshire Record Office.

If I have left anyone inadvertently out of the list, I apologise for the omission although their input was much appreciated.

Geraint Lloyd Owen, June Jones and Malcolm Lewis of Gwasg y Bwthyn, Caernarfon, and all their staff have been supportive and guided me through the publication with good humour.

My husband Elwyn has, as always, been a rock of support and understands my personal need to put the happy Llangwyfan Family in the public domain.

PREFACE by T H Evans, Head Gardener [1943-1973]
[Translation of an interview given in Welsh in Volume I – December 2008]

THE NORTH WALES SANATORIUM 1916-1951
RE-NAMED LLANGWYFAN HOSPITAL 1952-1981

To give its full official name – King Edward VII Welsh National Memorial Association with Headquarters in Cardiff.

During his reign it was said that King Edward VII expressed some concern regarding the ill health of his subjects who suffered from "Tuberculosis", and this is likely to be one of the reasons for creating a charter in his memory. The late Dr Glyn Penrhyn Jones in his book "Starvation & Pestilence in Wales" – [Dr Jones worked at the Sanatorium – 1955-59] talks about choosing a site in the Vale of Clwyd and the rather unique way in which it was chosen, the Association had decided to locate one sanatorium in the North and one in the South – that was at Talgarth. Sir D S Davies MP bought Plas Llangwyfan farm and donated it to the Memorial Association in memory of his father-in-law, Thomas Gee of Denbigh.

In 1916 the establishment was opened with 110 beds, after that there were many extensions to the buildings, amongst them a children's ward of 50 beds (Surgical Block) with Sir D S Davies's daughter (Mrs Lewis) contributing to the costs, also in the face of the intense hold that T.B. had taken, attempts were made to establish clinics throughout the length and breadth of Wales. The fact that a Sanatorium was to be built in the Vale of Clwyd was not accepted without contention, because this disease was dreaded in these parts as this region was reckoned to be comparatively healthy. I understand that developments were considerably affected by the First World War, but nevertheless things did progress gradually. There was only a limited response by local people to go to work on the project, although many local farmers had a lot of haulage work with horses and carts as the building work progressed.

Many young women from South Wales and Ireland came to serve as orderlies and nurses, some married local men, and some of the families remain in the area to this day. This also started the process of "Anglicizing" or "Irishizing" a Welsh community and gradually the local population accepted that the establishment and its surrounding environment was here to stay, although that certain fear attached to T.B. remained for many years to come.

In 1930 the Association purchased the Vron Yw estate – comprising – the Hall, the houses and 264 acres, here was the official residence of the Medical Superintendent from then on. The farm now amounted to approximately 500 acres and produced potatoes, cabbage, carrots, turnips, these were delivered to the Sanatorium daily as required as well as fresh milk from 50-60 milking cows.

During the 1930's there were approximately 275 patients (including 50 children), and in January 1941 another part of the hospital was opened with 150 beds, and this was called Llangwyfan Emergency Hospital. These were Hutments, to meet the effects of the war, the patients of the Hutments were all men. By 1952, when the name Sanatorium was changed to Llangwyfan Hospital, a change was taking place in the prescribed treatments due to the advent of new drugs, and also by now other disorders were being treated at the hospital.

Many of the patients came from all different parts of Wales, in particular from the South Wales valleys, Caernarfonshire, Wrexham and many from Anglesey, with a variety of ages, some of the youngest being women from the South Wales valleys, and it was said at the time that the prevailing social circumstances within that particular region of Wales probably accounted for this ie poverty, housing conditions, etc.

Friday was the day for "admittance" and a mini-bus which could carry 10 people would go to Denbigh Station, to meet the train, and because it was a yellow colour it became known as the "Banana Boat".

The period of stay for individual patients varied enormously during 1930's and 40's as rest and fresh air was prescribed and six months was a relatively short stay.

The doctor on the Block (Ward 4 and Ward 6) graded the patients every week. The purpose of grading, was that a small task was undertaken and if the patient graded higher from week to week, you could draw the conclusion that they were improving, although achieving the top grade did not always lead to going home, at times it could mean surgery.

During the early years, there were no windows with glass in them on the wards or cubicles only wooden shutters similar to "Louvre Shutters" and it was said that when it snowed the snow blew in and onto the beds.

It was in 1936 that they started refurbishing Blocks 3 and 4 which included fitting windows and heating, and in the following years, particularly when Dr Hawkins came in 1940 extensive improvements were carried out to all the buildings.

The Sanatorium was officially opened on 16th July 1920 by the then Monarch, King George V together with Queen Mary and Princess Mary, all schoolchildren within the local area had a special holiday for that day. I attended a school about 3 miles from Llangwyfan and like many others I was on a wall in the field opposite the hospital entrance to watch the King and the procession going past. The King was travelling by train to Denbigh Station and afterwards by car together with his considerable entourage. There were banners and bunting everywhere and there was a considerable display of pomp and splendour.

Accordingly I witnessed the opening and closing of Llangwyfan Hospital.

14

CHAPTER 1

A TALE OF TALGARTH AND LLANGWYFAN

PW was born in Aberystwyth, on the 9th April 1937, where his father had a greengrocers business in Thespian Street and took his van to sell fruit and vegetables to outlying villages. Peter attended North Road School and was then a pupil at Ardwyn Grammar School which I had attended and left before Peter's day.

In 1952 the Mass Miniature Radiology Unit (MMR) visited Ardwyn where all the pupils aged 14 years and older were X-rayed. Out of the total number of pupils investigated 3 had to return for further X-ray examination. At this time Peter's only symptom was a slight irritating cough clearing his throat, but no phlegm. He was found to have a Tuberculous lesion in the upper lobe of his right lung and was referred to the Chest Physician in Aberystwyth General Hospital; Dr G O Thomas.

He was put on the waiting list to be admitted to Talgarth Sanatorium and told that he should remain in bed until he was called, being allowed to get up for the toilet and to wash only. That was the end of his school days and he had no further school lessons. Before he was diagnosed he had two close friends who lived nearby and on hearing the diagnosis one immediately finished the friendship due to family pressure, Peter thought, as there was a stigma attached to Tuberculosis. The other came to see him every day for a chat and their friendship has lasted a lifetime, with them continuing to speak on the phone every week.

Having been diagnosed in October 1952 he was admitted to Talgarth on his 16th birthday, on the 9th April 1953.

Peter told me that he was not an academic and it was probably a good thing that he did not have to sit an examination such as O-levels, as he was scraping his way through school. I did not agree with this self-assessment.

When he got to Talgarth he was asked what his interests were and said Agriculture and he was advised to start an Agriculture Correspondence Course. In Talgarth there were 3 classes of bed patients:- B1 was complete bed rest, B2 were allowed to get up once a day to go the toilet and B3 were allowed up to go the toilet and wash as they wanted. He was classified as B3 and was there for 3-6 months in a cubicle by himself, part of a row of cubicles; as he described "all alone in a crowd", although he could see other patients. One side of the cubicle was glass and thus was open most of the time but he was not allowed to go outside.

When he graduated to getting up he was allowed to do so for ½ hour a day for the first week. Then ½ hour twice a day for a week. He had a weekly medical examination and as long as this was satisfactory he could do more the following week. When he was up for 6-8 hours a week he started on the next grade which was walking. At first, this was ½ mile in the morning, then ½ mile twice a day and over the next few months he got up to 3 miles twice a day. Meals were taken in the ward when he was allowed up and when he was up all day they were taken in the communal Dining Room. "If he wanted seconds at meal times he had to raise his arm and plate and Nurse would then come and fill it".

All patients were given a number and his was 58. He had his own thermometer and utensils. Before he took his temperature he dipped the thermometer in Euthymol (a mild antiseptic) and he then told the nurse what it was for her to record in a book – 98.4°F. Patients started occupational therapy once they had been able to walk 3 miles twice daily. He remembers making lamp shades for table lamps and also making an old Ardwynian scarf. This was the time also to start the working grades of which there were six:-

1st   After seeing Dr Ross, Medical Superintendent, he was told to take a small basket and carry out weeding.

2nd   Take a larger basket and hoe.

3rd   Clean the wards and windows.

4th   Given a spade and told to dig, with medical permission.

5th   Prepare the drive for tarmaccing.

6th   Use a horse and cart, the most difficult task, being to catch the horse first.

After all these tasks had been accomplished, he was assessed by Dr Ross who advised him to have surgery as he was young and this would ensure a complete cure. He accepted the advice and waited in a different block in Talgarth for the call to go to Sully Hospital. He was 22nd on the list, then after a few weeks he heard there were 3 patients returning from Sully so he moved to 19th, and this continued until he was top of the list which took months. The biggest lesson he learnt was that of patience.

He was admitted to Sully under the care of Mr Dilwyn Thomas to a receiving ward on the first floor. The Hospital had been constructed so that most patients had a view of the sea and he liked that. Boys were one side of the Hospital and girls the other, but they could see each other and communicated by spelling out with their hands; "I Love U". He had no idea of their names! He also got involved in playing discs on the Hospital Radio. He was then moved in turn to the Surgical Ward. On 17th March 1955 he was scheduled to a have a segmental resection of his right upper lobe, was prepared for surgery, given his pre-medication of

Omnopon and was about to get on a trolley to go to the Operating Theatre, when a Theatre Nurse rushed in and told him his operation was cancelled. He slept for most of the day and fortunately surgery was carried out the following day by Mr Probert. He has no idea who the Anaesthetist was.

He recovered in the Postoperative Ward which was at the top of the Hospital. He remembers that his chest drain was connected to an underwater suction apparatus. He was lying on his left side and the Physiotherapist came to move his right arm over his head to touch the bed-head. This was extremely painful, as was the removal of the suction tube 3-4 days later.

He returned to the Surgical Ward but things were not straight forward as the right lung was not expanding correctly due to an air leak. He was screened and it was decided he should have an oleothorax. Dr Fleming (grandson of Alexander Fleming – discoverer of Penicillin) marked his right upper chest, injected local anaesthesia into skin and tissues and then injected oil into the appropriate area to encourage adhesions to close the hole. He has no recollection if this was painful. His bed was elevated on 12" high blocks to raise the feet and during the day he spent 1 hour on his stomach, 1 hour on his right side and 1 hour on his back in rotation, he slept on his right side. This rotation went on for 6 weeks. Then he was allowed to get up and after a short time he returned to Talgarth, when he started again on the grades and after he was up for 8 hours he started walking, but not work. He was in Talgarth in total for 2 years and six months in Sully, leaving for home aged 18½ years feeling he had been very lucky.

He had been asked in Sully whether he would take part in a research project, having spirometry carried out before and after surgery and had readily agreed. He had an injection of a local anaesthetic into his trachea, a tube was passed into it through the mouth and he was attached to the Spirometer to test his lung function. It was very sore and uncomfortable. He got home and thought he'd escaped the postoperative test but he had a letter asking him to go back for it, which he did – to Sully, not an easy journey. He also had a letter asking him to go to Swansea prior to admission for National Service. He wrote back giving his health history but was told that he had to attend. When he got to Swansea he was examined and told that as he had had Tuberculosis he was not eligible for National Service – what bureaucracy!

He did not make any permanent friends in Talgarth. He remembers Jim Raw Rees, an Auctioneer in Aberystwyth being there at the same time as him. He also remembers lads having Artificial Pneumothorax (AP) and Pneumoperitoneum (PP) and going for refills of air once a week. Occasionally, a patient would have a phrenic crush where the phrenic nerve in the neck is crushed so that the diaphragm is paralysed and rises making the lung on that side collapse.

Peter was given Streptomycin in Talgarth:

> 3 months of Streptomycin and PAS
> 3 months of Streptomycin and 1NAH
> 3 months of PAS and 1NAH

Steptomycin was very painful and given deeply into the gluteal muscle, Nurse being gowned, gloved and masked. On one occasion the end of the needle touched the sciatic nerve, giving pain and a high temperature. Because he did not want to admit this and sent back to the beginning of the treatment he fiddled the result to make it normal.

Some patients on B1 and B2 had the foot of their bed raised on blocks to decrease the size of the thorax and collapse the lung and could be like this for months. The highest blocks were 12", they then came down to 4"-6" and later they were removed and they lay flat. Patients learnt to accept a change of pace of life. He only once felt "down" and the Night Sister talked to him. The camaraderie of patients was also helpful. Herbert Williams, the author of "A Severe Case of Dandruff" was born in Aberystwyth and Peter felt he had given an accurate account of life in a Sanatorium for an adolescent in this his first novel.

After he left Talgarth he attended the Chest Clinic in Aberystwyth. Dr G O Thomas asked him what he wanted to do, and he replied farming. He was told he was not strong enough for this and it was suggested that nursing might interest him in a Hospital outside Denbigh. He attended for an interview in Llangwyfan Hospital conducted by Miss Blodwen Morris (Matron) and Miss Kate Williams (Nursing Tutor). He was asked if it was his intention to take his State Registered Nurse (SRN) examination after completing his British Tuberculosis Association (BTA) and wanting to please, with no idea as to what it entailed, he said yes.

The BTA course took 2 years in 2 parts. Out of the 8 who tried only one passed first time. After 3-6 months he was allowed to try again and was successful. By this time he did not want to do his SRN but Matron Morris insisted that he went for an interview to Clatterbridge Hospital. As he had passed the BTA he did not have to sit part I (prelims). He gained his SRN after 18 months and returned to Llangwyfan as a Staff Nurse for 2 years. He joined the Royal College of Nursing – men only being allowed to join in 1961/62 and met other men who had joined the Ruthin and Denbigh Branch such as Sid Badland, the Chief Mental Nurse and Norman Hughes, Tutor in the North Wales Hospital for Nervous Diseases in Denbigh, commonly called "Denbigh Mental". In the meantime he had married Winnie, and asked Matron Morris for promotion. He also asked Sid Badland if there were jobs in Denbigh Mental Hospital and was told there were. Consequently, he did Registered Mental Nursing training and after qualifying, applications were invited from male nurses to work in the female wards as a trial and he was made a Deputy Sister. Three men held this position. They were resented by some of the Sisters because they had their SRN, but the rest of the staff welcomed them.

In 1966 he became a Charge Nurse on Elwy (female) Ward at Denbigh Mental Hospital where there were disturbed patients. It was an Admission Ward for disturbed patients with chronic Schizophrenia and he worked with Dr Mabel Tannahill on behaviour modification. The report on this compiled by Dr Tannahill and Dr Higson in 1985 points out that despite the uninspiring atmosphere on the ward, the staff morale was reasonably good and this was entirely due to the personality of the Charge Nurse, Peter Wilson, who besides having great talent for dealing with disturbed patients, genuinely liked them and was tolerant of their behaviour at all times. He was on the Appointments Committee for a Research Psychologist when Peter Higson was appointed. He is now the Chief Executive of the Health Inspectorate for Wales.

He left the Hospital in 1979 to become a Community Psychiatrist Nurse (CPN) in Wrexham, moving to Rhyl later to work in the resettlement team. This post entailed home visiting, counselling for marital and psychosexual problems, and giving advice on medication to keep people out of Denbigh Mental. When he worked in Holywell he came across Dr Gruff Penrhyn Jones whom he had baby-sat when his father was Deputy Superintendent of Llangwyfan.

He retired in 1993 aged 56 and took up volunteering. He was with the Samaritans for 2 years which he found frustrating as the service was often abused. In 1996 he started the Parish Magazine in Llandyrnog entitled "Village Voice". He had got the writing bug after attending Manchester Polytechnic in 1982 as part of community nursing studies for his CPN work. He took 12 months off to do this and was then upgraded to Nursing Officer. Bishop John Davies was then Rector of Llandyrnog and though supportive warned him that to produce a magazine once a month was a commitment, but he was happy doing it and for its 100th edition he invited Bishop John to contribute. IIe has sent copies of all the magazines to the National Library.

He and Winnie had three children, two girls and a boy who died aged 15 years. His two daughters are married and they have two grandchildren.

Peter is a gentle giant who works tirelessly for his community; a survivor of Tuberculosis and family tragedy without bitterness. A doer and helper who was the first to offer to sell "Llangwyfan"!

CHAPTER 2

TUBERCULOSIS OF THE SPINE
IN THE 1950's

As a schoolgirl "I" had been ill at home for 2 years with Rheumatic Fever, Pleurisy and back pain. She developed a pleural effusion and was referred to the Royal Alexandra Hospital, Rhyl and had the effusion drained by Dr Kraus, a Registrar to Dr D E Meredith. Two years later because of increasing back pain she was referred by Dr John Griffiths, her General Practitioner to see Dr McLeod, another General Practitioner in the practice, who had experience of orthopaedics and he requested an X-ray. He referred her to the Chest Clinic in Edward Henry Street, Rhyl where she was seen by Dr J Morrison and Tuberculosis of the spine was diagnosed. She was sent home to bed and seen by a Health Visitor from Abergele who told her that she would have a 3-4 month wait for a bed in Llangwyfan.

Her mother, a widow, was concerned about her daughter and went to seek advice from the Minister of the Chapel they attended, who said he would go and see a friend of his, G O Williams who was Vice-Chairman of Clwyd and Deeside Hospital Management Committee and Huw T Edwards, the Chairman. Within a week she was admitted to Llangwyfan Hospital and put to bed in a corner position in Block 7, which had windows behind and to the side of the bed. Block 7 had two Wards and a total of 28 beds under the control of Sister Griffiths and she was told that she had the best bed. G O Williams would visit her when he went to Llangwyfan.

At first she was assessed and measured, and the carpenter came to make a frame around her body. Approximately 2 weeks after admission when everything was prepared she was taken to the Plaster Room for an hour and a half with half a dozen people in the room, and was placed naked on a theatre-style metal table balancing on her abdomen and head, with her arms hanging down and being supported. Sheets of Plaster of Paris were dipped in big bowls of warm water and these were then placed on her back and everyone smoothed it down her back, but not further forward than her arms. When sufficient Plaster of Paris had been applied it was lifted off like a shell to dry. Afterwards the joiner put it in the frame which had been prepared. The inside of the shell was lined with cotton wool. This was then put on a Gobowen Bed which was approximately 7 foot long and had 4 wheels. The frame was put on top of the bed mattress. The head of the bed was lifted so that the head lay higher than the body and feet. A wooden board was placed behind the soles of the feet to keep them in place. She could not lift her head as a band was placed across it with weights on each side, to keep it straight.

The middle of the mattress was slid out for toileting. No explanation was given beforehand but everyone was very kind and she made up her mind that she just had to get on with it and put up with the discomfort. This was worse during the hours of darkness when she would long to turn over and lie on her side – "for just five minutes", but that of course was impossible. Gradually, the discomfort eased and became bearable, and again when she was lifted out of her plaster bed, for two or three nights, she actually longed to go back to it. After she emptied her bowels, the Nurse would clean her up with what was like tow or kemp which had been put in warm water to soften it. She had started menstruating before becoming a patient and she had to manage the sanitary towels herself. "It was horrible".

She was the youngest in a Ward with 7 or 8 other girls, two of them were in plaster beds, the others had Tuberculosis of the kidneys or glands but not lungs. Her plaster was changed every 6 months and she remained in this position for 18 months in total. After 3 months she was taken out of the bed and rolled over to have a bath, then returned to the bed which had clean cotton wool on the plaster and sheets. Mr Norman Roberts, her Consultant, visited every 3 months and she was X-rayed one week before he came.

Finally after coming out of the plaster bed, she was kept bed-ridden for 2-3 weeks in a plaster jacket which was applied immediately she came out of bed. She was then gradually allowed to sit up in bed and then to put her legs over the edge of the mattress. At first, her legs were very painful and she was told not to do this for a few days and then try again. Then she found she could do it without pain and was allowed to sit out in a chair.

The first 10 days in the plaster bed were very painful and uncomfortable but analgesics were not given. She started on PAS and Streptomycin on admission. PAS was given by mouth 4-5 times a day and was horrible. She could not drain the dose in one gulp and before the next gulp would start retching. Because of this she was put on Rimifon, one tablet a day, after a week. She was also given Streptomycin into the front of the top of her legs which resulted in lumps appearing. She had 3 months of PAS and Streptomycin followed by 3 months of Rimifon and Streptomycin, then 2 weeks of no drugs before the cycle restarted.

Three months after she got out of the plaster bed she was sent home. Just before going she was measured for a back support which was of iron and leather and had 3 lots of straps to keep it in place across the shoulders, hips and waist. "It was torture". She did not have to return to Llangwyfan but had a chest X-ray a year later. She remembers Mr Norman Roberts, the Ortho-paedic Surgeon from Liverpool, as a very nice, tall handsome man with white hair and very blue eyes. He would always check her X-rays.

She was too old to attend the School, there was no entertainment and she could not leave her bed. She was not unhappy for the day was structured with something happening in regular sequence. A cup of tea to wake up, followed by cleaning hands and face with a wet flannel. After breakfast there was the medicine round, then the bed was tidied and at 11:00 am a rest hour. She found the time passed quite quickly with chat, reading or listening to the radio.

Her mother visited once a fortnight on a Sunday, alternating with her brother. She had 3 changes of bus to get there after first going to Chapel, then home for tea and bread and butter. She said the return buses were good in waiting for visitors.

Once she was mobile she was expected to wash herself but was not allowed to do any housework duties. In 1958 she started work, the hard slog behind her.

CHAPTER 3

THE PULMONARY LABORATORY

Following the publication of "Llangwyfan" in 2007, interest was expressed in the picture of the Pulmonary Laboratory showing various pieces of complex apparatus that were being used. The Pulmonary Lab was introduced quite late in the history of the sanatorium, which, for the first 40 years of its existence cared for patients with tuberculosis mainly affecting the lungs or the bones. During this time pulmonary TB was diagnosed by a combination of tests based on the patient's medical history, physical examination of the chest, chest X-ray and, at best, growing tubercle bacilli from patient samples. From the 1920s to 1960s a physiological, or functional, assessment of the lung was not part of the diagnostic process mainly because, at that time, the science of lung physiology was only slowly developing. Any assessment of lung function was confined to seeing how well a patient could walk up stairs or, if too disabled, how far could they walk on the flat. The treatment of pulmonary TB in this period was almost entirely centred on rest, either by keeping the patients in bed or, more drastically, by resting the affected lung either by surgically removing part of the rib cage on that side, interfering with the movement of the diaphragm or collapsing the lung itself. All of these surgical procedures reduced the volume of air in the lung and sometimes made breathing more difficult but it was not the practice at the time to use physiological tests to measure this change in lung function.

Another factor that slowed the use of pulmonary function tests was that in many TB patients the infection within the lung, although easily seen on the X-ray, affected only a small part of the lung and reduced the volume of air in the lung only by a small amount. Pulmonary TB in humans is usually seen in the top part of the lung; interestingly bats also get pulmonary TB, but because they spend much of their time hanging upside down, they get TB infection in the bottom of the lung. This is explained because TB organisms grow best in high oxygen concentrations. There is more oxygen in whatever part of the lung is uppermost because less blood flows to the uppermost part of the lung consequently less oxygen is taken from the upper lung into the blood than in the lower part of the lung. Patients with much more extensive disease progress to severe scarring of large parts of the lung that causes lung fibrosis and severely reduces pulmonary function. Reduction in lung volume also happened if TB affected the upper spine causing a deformity, which would also affect the ribs attached to that part of the spine.

The Second World War saw the introduction of anti-TB drugs and coincidentally led to the rapid development of pulmonary physiology as a spin off from wartime aviation medicine. It now became possible to measure the volume of air in the lung in different diseases although initially this was almost entirely confined to research laboratories. One of the biggest of these in the UK was in Wales at the MRC Pneumoconiosis Research Unit in Llandough Hospital, Penarth. Set up in 1945 this was concerned with the different effects of coal (mines) and stone dust (quarries). A very elaborate set of equipment was assembled for pulmonary function testing but almost none of this spilled over into the clinical side of chest medicine until the late 1950s and 60s. When it did there were several important aspects of lung physiology that needed to be measured. For example the measurement of the volume of air being breathed in and out (the Tidal Volume) was technically easy but in addition the clinicians also wanted to know the volume of air in the lungs themselves and how quickly this could be breathed in and out. This was because diseases like asthma, bronchitis and emphysema caused airway obstruction and this was the main cause of breathlessness. Measuring the volume of residual air in the lung itself needed some slightly more complicated apparatus than simply measuring the tidal volume and expiratory flow rate.

Brian Cowlishaw began to set up the Llangwyfan Pulmonary lab in 1959. Until that time no such lab existed at the sanatorium. Initially he worked under the direction of Mr Walter Portwood who had been an Industrial Chemist but, unfortunately, his industrial expertise was not well suited to setting up a pulmonary laboratory and later, in 1963, Dr Biagi arranged for him to go to the Brompton Chest Hospital in London for 6 weeks to learn the appropriate choice of equipment and techniques. The Llangwyfan lab was first set up in the old plaster room in Hut E and then moved next to the Pathology laboratory in what was the Nurses School.

Fig 1

The picture in "Llangwyfan" of the Pulmonary Lab shows a spirometer in the foreground and another one in the background. The spirometer is a miniature version of the old fashioned gasometer. The diagram (Fig 1) shows how the spirometer was used to measure lung function. With a patient breathing quietly through the tube, the inside chamber of the spirometer moves up and down, as shown by the double ended arrow, and this movement, the Tidal Volume, is recorded with a pen which draws a line on a sheet of graph paper which is marked in litres and millilitres. The spirometer is partly filled with water that prevents the expired air escaping. If, instead of recording normal resting Tidal Volume, we ask the subject to first take a maximum breath in and then slowly breath all the way out this measures the Vital Capacity. We can also test for airways obstruction as in asthma, bronchitis, cystic fibrosis or emphysema; if the subject breathes all the way in then blows out as fast as possible the volume of air blown out in 1 second is the forced expiratory volume or FEV1.0.

After a maximum expiration there is still air left in the lung. This is called the Residual Volume. This changes in a characteristic way in different lung diseases and to measure this requires a modification to this spirometer system. It is obvious from the diagram that if the subject goes on breathing in and out of the spirometer the oxygen will be used up and replaced by carbon dioxide. This becomes unpleasant and difficult so carbon dioxide can be removed using granules of soda lime, used every day by anaesthetists during surgery, and a small amount of oxygen run in to replace this will keep the volume of the air in the spirometer constant. To measure the residual volume of air in the lung a small volume of helium is also added and allowed to mix with the air in the circuit. The final concentration of helium is measured with a simple device called a katharometer and the result used to calculate the residual volume. The rate with which the helium mixes with the air in the lung is also used as a measurement of the mixing efficiency of the lung. In airways obstruction the mixing efficiency is nearly always reduced.

An important further development of this breathing circuit was used to measure the efficiency with which oxygen diffused from the small lung airways and alveoli into the blood. This is reduced in emphysema and lung fibrosis where the surface area of the lung, normally the size of a tennis court, is reduced in size. Because it is technically difficult to measure the diffusion of oxygen a very small concentration of carbon monoxide is used instead. This test is called the carbon monoxide diffusing capacity or Lung Transfer factor. In the original volume of Llangwyfan (2007) there is a photograph of a large white apparatus shown in the laboratory that was used for this test. When this was developed it was a pioneering time and many experiments were needed to refine the method and ensure that it was giving accurate results.

Measuring the volume of air in the lung is important and a quicker way of doing this without breathing in and out of a spirometer is by using a whole body plethysmograph. In this method the patient sits inside a large airtight box with a clear Perspex door. The patient breaths through a tube that is suddenly obstructed for a few seconds and the change in pressure in the tube and the box are measured. The two pressures are displayed on an oscilloscope and the volume calculated. This sounds quite complicated but Brian constructed his own plethysmograph with the aid of the hospital carpenter who made a wooden box fitted with a Perspex panel.

So far techniques have been described for measuring lung ventilation and gas diffusion. Because the purpose of the lungs is to extract oxygen from the air and exchange this for carbon dioxide one of the priorities was to be able to measure the amount of oxygen and carbon dioxide in the gas being breathed in and out. It was also important to know what the concentrations of these gases were in the blood. So "Gas Analysis"

Figure 2 – Lab equipment

was an important technical step when setting up the pulmonary laboratory. The following section describes how he did this at Llangwyfan.

The above photograph (Fig 2) shows an array of equipment that was needed to measure the concentration of oxygen and carbon dioxide in the respired gas as well as the patients' blood. Nowadays it is technically very easy to measure these entities, in fact the methods are so reliable and simple that anaesthetists routinely monitor all these variables continuously in every patient during surgery. It was quite a different story from the 1960s until the lab eventually closed. Brian was an experienced photographer who developed his own films and there are photographs of nearly all the early equipment that he used to measure these gas concentrations.

When Dr Owen visited Brian to talk about the lab she saw a

small white wooden box on his desk (Fig 3). This was an oxygen meter that he designed using pyrogallol to absorb oxygen in a series of glass tubes and syringes. This was used for many years until an electronic oxygen meter was purchased. Also shown in the above picture is the traditional Van Slyke apparatus for measuring carbon dioxide. Analysis of arterial blood samples with electronic methods gradually developed beginning with measurements of the acidity of blood, the pH, as well as carbon dioxide and oxygen saturation. The photograph shows the complex water bath system in Perspex boxes that were needed to keep the temperature during the analysis very close to body heat. Initially very large samples, 20ml, were needed and it was too difficult to measure oxygen pressure in blood samples. Later in the 1980s these were replaced with electronic methods.

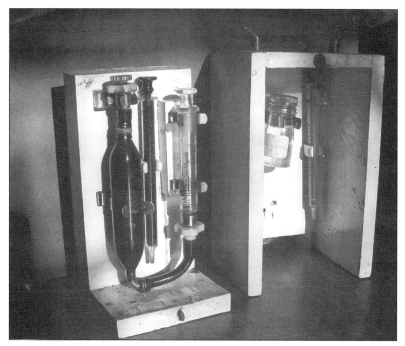

Fig 3 – Oxygen Analyzer

Many of the tests were done as part of routine clinical management but later on a research project was set up in collaboration with University College of North Wales, Bangor. This focussed on trying to identify the gases formed in grain silos but they did not achieve any significant results. It was believed that various oxides of nitrogen including nitrogen dioxide (NO_2) were the toxic gases. In 1967 Dr Biagi and Dr Bapat became interested in farmers lung in the chest clinics of Bangor, Abergele, Holywell, Wrexham, Denbigh and Shrewsbury between Ist January 1958 and 31st December 1967. Ninety-five patients were studied. They found that pulmonary function was significantly altered with the carbon monoxide diffusion being most affected. They concluded that continued exposure to mouldy hay without wearing a mask was the most important factor responsible as nitrogen dioxide was released above decomposing grain or silage in the confined space of the silos. They also showed a defect in oxygen and carbon dioxide exchange caused by obstruction in small airways. The disease was 20 times more common in the areas with the highest rainfall. They advised farmers to wear masks when working with mouldy hay.

When Llangwyfan closed all the apparatus in the Pulmonary Laboratory was sent to Glan Clwyd Pathology Lab.

CHAPTER 4

COPING WITH AN EMERGENCY – 1960's

Closure of Main Operating Theatre in the
Royal Alexandra Hospital, Rhyl

In the late 1960's just before the Annual Christmas Dance an emergency occurred in the main Operating Theatre of the Royal Alexandra Hospital [RAH] necessitating its immediate closure for 2-3 months for fumigation, deep cleaning and painting. The plan was immediately put into effect to cope with this unexpected occurrence. Emergencies were dealt with in the Endoscopy Theatre (as it was called) which was much smaller. All patients on the waiting list were screened and "cold" cases, which were not likely to cause any problems, were diverted to Llangwyfan Hospital for surgery.

Three days were set aside every week in Llangwyfan to deal with these patients, the same number being dealt with each day, as would have been in the RAH. Patients were sent for by the Secretary a week to 10 days beforehand. At the same time a list of the patients sent for was sent to the Theatre Nursing Sister in charge. The Sister delegated to go to Llangwyfan would choose the instruments which were to be used on each patient and these would be autoclaved in packs for each individual and sent in advance. Patients were admitted the day before surgery and assessed by the junior staff of the particular Surgeon. Monday was for Mr O M Jonathan, Tuesday for Mr Owen Daniel and Friday for Mr Edward Wood.

The fumigation work on the RAH Theatre started immediately with Formaldehyde when the whole Theatre was sealed off for a week until the door was opened when a horrible smell leaked out. Then the Theatre was cleaned from top to bottom with 1% Hibitane solution by the nurses and technicians and left for a couple of days. It was then dry mopped and the cycle of washing and drying repeated. Floors were washed with Lysol.

Sister Emma Jane Scott, a senior Operating Department Nursing Sister was in charge. She left her home in Prestatyn at 7:30 am to go to Rhyl to pick up a Student Nurse from Dolawen and they would arrive in Llangwyfan between 8:00 - 8:30 am to prepare the Theatre for the list to start at 9:30 am and continue until 3:00 pm. She would then see that the Theatre was cleared and left about 4:30 pm to go back to Rhyl to the RAH. She remembers two hazards on the journey; snow and floods, and as these were often in the dark they caused an unexpected shock. At first she went to Llangwyfan via Denbigh and found the road signage was good. Then she found the road back via Bodfari and Trefnant and found it a better way. She has a recollection of seeing the almond trees in bloom between Bodfari and Trefnant at the side of a long straight road. Returning to Rhyl she sometimes had to deal with emergencies and the day she hit the flood near the Oriel House Hotel in St Asaph the water came over the bonnet of her mini, but there was no time to delay as she was expected in the RAH.

She did not have to clean the Theatre at Llangwyfan, as this was done by their staff, apart from the instruments of which she was in charge. She remembers the very large sterilizing room in Llangwyfan with a sterilizer which belched out steam. The Operating Theatre had a glass roof and she had to keep moving the Mayo table on which she had placed her instruments in order to avoid drips from condensation.

She remembers the static operating theatre light, confirming this observation from Dr A A Khalil, an Anaesthetist from Rhyl; that the operating table had to be moved so that the light was on the incision or deeper in the body.

The operating theatre lists were well planned and all the patients had their surgery carried out. This was unlike her personal experience this year (2007) when she fell and fractured her neck of femur and was admitted on a Monday for surgery later that day and starved; to be told later by the Surgeon that they had run out of theatre time and she would have to wait for another day. She told me that she had exploded and told the Surgeon that in her day, lists were always finished and planned better, and they never ever ran out of theatre time. And, she said, when she eventually had surgery she had a sore throat and a broken tooth. She said it wasn't fair on elderly patients in their 80's and 90's (she is now 90 years of age) to be day patients. She has had considerable problems with her fracture and the last time she was admitted she had to ring at 4:00 pm on Sunday to make sure there was a bed and was admitted at 5:00 pm for further surgery on the Tuesday.

She said she saw a former Matron on the ward who insisted that she be called Miss G. She, herself, hadn't been asked what she wanted to be called and was called Emma, but later a District Nurse had telephoned her to apologise for not asking her beforehand as to what she wanted to be called.

I recall Miss Christine Evans, Urological Surgeon, saying during her delivery of the Ivor Lewis Memorial Lecture (2007) that she insisted that her nursing staff called her Miss Evans, and as a Contestant on the television quiz programme, the Weakest Link, insisting that Anne Robinson also called her Miss Evans. At her second attempt Miss Evans was the winner.

Half way through her time in Llangwyfan one of Sister Scott's fingers was crushed between the theatre trolley and table. Mr Ivor Lewis put ribbon gauze around her finger and told her to wear 2 pairs of gloves to carry on. She also fell over a bench which had been left outside theatre and hurt her leg which was followed 3 weeks later by thrombosis, so she had sick leave and her place taken by Sister Anne Pye. She remembers that time as a happy time when everyone worked hard and pulled together.

At first she was scared of Mr Ivor Lewis but she learnt to understand him and learnt from him. On one occasion she worked through the night with Mr Lewis and Dr Goronwy Owen as the Anaesthetist, with emergencies being dealt with during the list. This meant that the list finished at 6:00 am the following day, then she had to clear up. She had worked 24 hours. Because Sister Gwen Jenkins who was in charge of the theatre was taken ill, she couldn't have the day off and finished her work at 3:00 pm. A marathon. She found Mr Lewis considerate and compassionate; a man with stamina. Once during a long list they found the houseman had gone to sleep, but Mr Lewis told her to leave him until he woke up.

She remembers Charge Nurse Jeff Davies, whose wife was Dr June Arnold's Secretary, and who moved to take charge of the Operating Theatres in Inverness Hospital, being told by the Surgeon that he was going to carry out an Ivor Lewis Operation and being very proud to be able to tell him that he had worked with Mr Ivor Lewis.

She got on well with Mr Owen Daniel who she felt treated everyone with respect; "you knew where you stood with him". She felt he worked with them and did his best for his patients. Mr Daniel liked quietness, solitude and peace, with time to think. He took a walk every day and also enjoyed his yacht. He was a big thinker and enjoyed research. We all remember the series of around 200 patients who had bile duct pressures carried out to find out if they had gall stones in the duct. If there were he would carry on to explore it. Also a dye was injected into the duct, followed by an X-ray. Every cholecystectomy had this procedure, the series taking 3-4 years, but none of these were carried out in Llangwyfan. As well as his scientific background

Mr Daniel was good with colour and line; a forthright man, on the side of the underdog.

Mr O M Jonathon was quite the opposite, very quiet and reserved who dealt with everyone in the same way. He was held in high regard by everyone and had carried out research on Hydatid Disease.

Sister Ann Pye (now Roche) applied for a post of Casualty Sister at the Royal Alexandra Hospital in 1965, but when she attended for interview she was told by the Matron, Miss Gordon, that the post had been filled but that there was a vacancy in the Operating Theatre. She explained she had no training other than during her general nurse training in this field, but as long as she could receive training she would take the post. She found that she really enjoyed the work and stayed until 1975. When she started, Sister Gwen Jenkins was in charge of the Royal Alexandra Hospital Operating Theatre but when the emergency occurred, Sister Hilda Knowles had gained this position and she remained in the Royal Alexandra Hospital. The remaining senior nursing staff were on the rota to go to Llangwyfan with Sister Pye in charge and reporting to Sister Knowles.

Sister Pye thought the Theatre in Llangwyfan was antiquated and could not believe they worked under such conditions. She has an abiding memory of the huge sterilizers giving off steam which condensed on the glass theatre roof and dripped down on the instruments which had been arranged on the Mayo table, which was moveable on castors. Although instruments from the Royal Alexandra Hospital were taken, some of the Llangwyfan instruments could be also used and care had to be taken at the end of each patient's surgery to separate these. She felt the Llangwyfan staff did not really like having them there.

The Royal Alexandra Hospital team worked well and she remembers Charge Nurse Jeff Davies and Charge Nurse John Redmond being there as well as Beryl Hughes (née Roberts) who gave long service to the Royal Alexandra Hospital Theatre and was an invaluable member. Sister Pye thought Llangwyfan a beautiful place but awful to get to, along narrow lanes. She always took the Bodfari route and would park her car near the Theatre. The staff would go to the dining room for meals which were very good. She remembers going around the Hospital and seeing a room full of Iron Lungs. I presume they were from other hospitals and stored in Llangwyfan, and wonder where they went when it closed.

She thought Ivor Lewis and Nancie Faux were Icons and it was an honour to have worked with them. She was petrified when she scrubbed for her first patient with Mr Lewis, but he was very nice and told her exactly what he wanted. When it came to closing the peritoneum she told him there was a swab missing, but he went on suturing and she continued frantically looking for it. Towards the end he stepped back from the table and there was the swab; great was her relief. He would often hide swabs in order to test the Theatre Staff. I think he did this to keep them all on their toes. I told her I thought this was good as I had once been called to go with him to another hospital where another surgeon had operated and a swab had indeed been left in the patient – fortunately without ill effect.

She enjoyed working with Mr Daniel and Mr Jonathan who had completely different personalities as has been mentioned, both being very good surgeons. She also mentioned Mr Daniel's bile duct pressure studies which could be a bit tense. She found that Dr Green and Dr Row, the Radiologists were very friendly with the staff when they had to come to the Theatre.

From her time in the Royal Alexandra Hospital Theatre she remembers weekends being labour intensive making swabs to use during surgery. "Pompoms" were rolled cotton wool balls, then put in a gauze sleeve so that they could be picked up by an instrument, "Pledgets" were cut strips of tape which were rolled to the right size, 5 then being put in a pack. Big drums were filled with these and autoclaved. Big packs of gauze were also put in packs of 5 and threaded with cotton to put in drums. Also at weekends all instruments were whitened with a white powder which was then rubbed off and polished so that they were sparkling clean and then autoclaved.

Albert, the Theatre Porter, would remove the glass panelling from the scrub up area every Saturday morning to be washed down on the Theatre Table. The Table would then be stripped and cleaned, together with the Theatre trolleys. Grandma's Lysol was used for washing the Theatre floors at the end of each list and between patients the floor would be mopped – this could be anyone's job.

Steve Cooper : A Senior Theatre Technician

Steve Cooper remembers working in Llangwyfan in 1974 when the Theatre Staff from the Royal Alexandra Hospital was transferred there for a short while, when the Operating Theatre in the Royal Alexandra was closed. He recollects it as being an interesting and challenging experience, which he enjoyed very much. His late wife had been a patient there for 12 months with Tuberculosis and had discussed life there at that time with Steve. She had contracted Tuberculosis whilst working in the North Wales Hospital; her sister, father and grandfather had also been patients at various times in Llangwyfan. Alan Rogers, his brother-in-law's wife Judith (Dickens), was a Staff Nurse in Llangwyfan for a few years. Her mother, Mrs Dickens, was a telephonist in Llangwyfan from 1958. Alan Rogers is now Head of Nursing, Surgery and Anaesthesia at Ysbyty Glan Clwyd.

In 1974 the Theatre in Llangwyfan was considerably under-used compared to its past and the Alexandra and Llangwyfan staff worked well together, becoming very efficient. Mr Daniel and Mr Jonathan had occasional lists in addition to Mr Howell Hughes and Mr Doyle.

Sister Pam Davies – d. 10 July 2008

Sister Pam Davies was the Ward Sister on the male surgical ward called "Duke Ward", in the Royal Alexandra Hospital. When she got to Llangwyfan she was put in charge of a medical ward with Dr Biagi's patients and after 2 weeks she complained because she wanted to look after the surgical patients who had been transferred from the Royal Alexandra. She said Dr Biagi was very nice and all his patients spoke very highly of him. She felt he provided a sanctuary for the chest patients who were in-patients during the winter months and that he was dedicated to his work. She had previously taken one of her children to see him when he developed asthma and he had assured her this would pass when he was 10 years old, as indeed it did.

She and Sister Judith Dickens ran the Surgical Ward together at first, then Sister Dickens moved to look after Mr Daniel's Ward on Block 7, whilst she stayed with Mr Jonathan. She remembered seeing me in the Operating Theatre when she took patients there and confirmed that surgery was busy and all sorts of operations carried out. She enjoyed the experience and thought they stayed 3 months. When they returned to the Royal Alexandra all staff had a welcome letter (opposite) back from Miss Magwen Williams, Principal Nursing Officer.

Another interesting historical item she showed me was the Programme for a Pantomime of Robin Hood which was put on in Llangwyfan on the 22nd December 1919. Her father's sister Maria Agnes Richards, was a patient there as a girl and she died aged 19 years. Her father never mentioned it as it was such a sad time for him, but she told me that he had been a marvellous father and indoctrinated her on how to lead a good life and to be grateful for each day.

42

PWYLLGOR RHEOLI YSBYTAI CLWYD A GLANNAU DYFRDWY
CLWYD AND DEESIDE HOSPITAL MANAGEMENT COMMITTEE

ROYAL ALEXANDRA HOSPITAL,
MARINE DRIVE,
RHYL Flintshire.

Tel. Rhyl 4631

Matron: Miss I. ~~~~~~~~~~~~~~ SRN
Miss D. M. GORDON SRN S.C.M.

Hospital Secretary:
W. M. COWX.

Our ref: MW/SC.

Your ref:

Date: 18th March, 1974.

Sister P. Davies.
Duke Ward,
Royal Alexandra Hospital,
RHYL.

Dear Sister Davies,

I wish to thank you and all your ward staff for your co-operation during the time your wards have been closed. I do realise what an upheaval it has been and how difficult it has been for those of you who have had to work at Llangwyfan, Colwyn Bay and Abergele.

I am sure you will all be very pleased to be back at the Royal Alexandra Hospital.

Yours sincerely,

M. Williams.
Principal Nursing Officer.

43

CHAPTER 5

NORTH WALES HOSPITAL
PATIENTS TRANSFER

In the 1960's the top huts in Llangwyfan were emptying due to the improved outlook for Tuberculosis patients. At the same time, large wards in the North Wales Hospital were being modernised and decorated with the number of patients in each ward being reduced. It was decided that it would be of mutual benefit to both hospitals to decant one ward of around 26 female patients from the North Wales Hospital to Llangwyfan so that their ward could be decorated, and it was envisaged this would be a short term agreement. This proved to have worked so well that it was decided to continue with the arrangement so that use could be made of an empty ward in Denbigh whilst others were being upgraded. It was a mutually satisfactory partnership on policy with Dr Gwynne Williams and Dr William Biagi (both Medical Superintendents in spirit if not in name), co-operating well together.

The patients were elderly, mentally infirm (EMI) who didn't go out and many did not get out of bed or dress. The medical staff who visited the patients were Registrars from the North Wales Hospital – Dr Kirby and Dr O'Toole. The female ward staff who transferred from Denbigh were very happy in Llangwyfan as supervision was lax and the patients easy to look after. Staff would be able to visit the Kinmel Arms, Llandyrnog and there was much clinking of bottles. In the mid 1970's alcohol was banned in the group hospitals as a result of an episode in the North Wales Hospital, when a patient at Christmas attacked a male Nurse who had to defend himself. A report was written and the patient confronted but he maintained that the Nurse smelt of alcohol and a lot of staff became afraid that if they smelt of alcohol their word would not be accepted. Consequently, Clwyd and Deeside HMC decided to ban alcohol from hospital premises.

The Night Superintendent from Denbigh, Charge Nurse Gwilym Hughes, visited two to three times a week. Two thirds of the senior nursing staff in Denbigh were male and they were whole-time. Many had married nurses and had families and when the wives returned to work they often did night work and were part-time becoming whole-time when their family had grown up. Many of these worked nights in Llangwyfan which was always short of staff. There were enough female staff to cover the EMI patients from Denbigh during the day but at night male staff visited.

Charge Nurse D B Jones visited when Charge Nurse G Hughes was on leave and said he had never been in such a cold place. Denbigh was always kept warm and it was a big contrast to go to Llangwyfan. Water froze on the inside of the windows and it would take all morning to get the heat up in the ward where these elderly patients were housed. At meal times the ward doors were open to let the food trolleys come in, letting more cold air enter as well, being shut as quickly as possible. Extra blankets had to be found to cover the patients. When Glan Clwyd opened DB Jones was admitted as an emergency during a cold snap and when he complained of the cold, extra blankets could not be found for the bed.

Some of these frail patients may have died from hypothermia but whose responsibility was their care? A Nursing Officer who was there when the weather was extreme went to complain to the Senior Psychiatric Nursing Officer in Denbigh, and in a week the ward was closed and the patients transferred back to the warmth of the North Wales Hospital.

Testimony – Charge Nurse D B Jones.

CHAPTER 6

VISITING NORTH WALES CONSULTANTS

Introduction

Prior to the start of the National Health Service in 1948 the medical service in this area of North Wales was run by General Practitioners (GP's) who referred patients needing major surgery and treatment mainly to Liverpool. Many GP's carried out surgery in Cottage Hospitals and became specialists in a minor way, and were very good Doctors. The first Consultant appointed by the Welsh Regional Hospital Board to Rhyl was Dr Pierce Williams, a General Practitioner with an interest in Radiology and the second, the whole time appointment of a Consultant Physician, Dr David Meredith, who started on the 1st August 1950. Other Consultant appointments followed including Mr Ivor Lewis, Consultant Surgeon and Dr Nancie Faux, Consultant Anaesthetist in 1951 who were based in Rhyl, and Dr E Clifford Jones as Consultant Chest Physician for Wrexham as well as Clwyd and Deeside HMC, who commenced on the 1st May 1951. There was already a Consultant Service in Wrexham and Bangor and many of these were available for consultation in the Rhyl area until the medical service there was established.

Honorary Consultants visited Llangwyfan from Liverpool and London and I have written previously about them. However, many Consultants appointed in North Wales went on to have distinguished careers. They were appointed by WRHB to an area controlled by Hospital Management Committees, and in the case of Rhyl would also visit Llangwyfan when invited to do so by the

Medical Superintendent. I have written about them in the account which follows so that their contribution to Llangwyfan and the development of the Health Service in North Wales is not forgotten. Because many Anaesthetists visited Llangwyfan I have gathered them together at the end of this chapter.

Dr E Clifford Jones
Consultant Chest Physician [1951-1974]

Dr E Clifford Jones was appointed Consultant Chest Physician to Wrexham and Clwyd & Deeside HMC on the 1st May 1951. He ran the Wrexham Chest Clinic at 18 Grosvenor Road which opened in 1946, replacing a Dispensary in Temple Row. In June 1943 when he was working in the Middlesex County Sanatorium, Clare Hall in Hertfordshire, he was a co-author of a paper on Pneumoperitoneum in the Collapse Therapy of Pulmonary Tuberculosis, giving a review of the literature on pneumoperitoneum, the technique used, complications, details of 10 cases and its place in the Collapse Therapy of Pulmonary Tuberculosis.

He had beds in Hut D in Llangwyfan until 1964 when it closed, and his patients were then moved to Block 6. Block 6 was a two-storey building for male patients with, at that time, some single rooms downstairs and upstairs had beds for acute chest patients on the one side and terminal/chronic patients on the other.

He retired in 1974 and had left the area before his successor, Dr Tim Baker, arrived on 1st January 1975. It was thought Dr Jones had family and that when he retired he moved back to the North East of England and did not keep in touch with his Wrexham friends. Dr Baker attended Llangwyfan to see his patients about once a month on a Friday afternoon when there was often a clinical meeting held which he attended. As the number of patients dwindled his visits became infrequent to see one or two patients.

Dr Baker thought that Dr Clifford Jones ran a very good tight service which he did not need to change when he arrived. He had beds in Acton Ward in the Maelor and his outpatient clinic was run from the Wrexham Chest Clinic. Dr Jones ran a direct X-ray reporting service from the Chest Clinic and any patient he thought should be seen was given a direct appointment to the clinic at the time of the X-ray Report. The Chest Clinic closed in 1984 when the Maelor Hospital opened and at that time the Radiology Department took over the reporting of all X-rays.

Dr E Clifford Jones was Chairman of the Wrexham Board of Post-graduate Studies from 1968-1971. He was obviously a reticent man but we can read testimony of the excellent service he provided to his patients and of his diagnostic skills. Sister Bella Hughes née Griffiths was a patient of his for two years and later joined the staff of Llangwyfan. She left when she got married, later taking her three children to Wrexham Chest Clinic to have BCG by Dr Clifford Jones

Dr Mary Gallagher

Dr Gallagher was appointed Senior Registrar in Llangwyfan on 5 October 1950, Mr Howell Hughes being appointed on to Committee which appointed her in an advisory capacity. Her initial salary was £1,000 per year with annual increments of £100 to a maximum of £1,300 and she paid for emoluments £150 per year. In 1951 she was appointed Deputy Medical Superintendent. She was a very good clinician and excellent with children. She bought and lived in a cottage between Tremeirchion and Bodfari but after she retired, she became confused and returned to live in Ireland with her family.

48

Dr June Arnold MD, FRCP
First Consultant Geriatrician [1961-1985]

Dr June Arnold was appointed Consultant Geriatrician by the Welsh Hospital Board in 1961 to initiate and provide a service for the elderly for the Clwyd and Deeside group of Hospitals. She had beds for in-patients in HM Stanley Hospital, St Asaph and Lluesty Hospital, Holywell – both old workhouses with dormitory provision for able-bodied people, reached by awkward stone staircases. She had a total of 194 beds, 149 at Lluesty and 45 at St Asaph. Lluesty housed patients for rehabilitation and long stay care as well as acute care. She organised the first respite care scheme in Wales, where patients were admitted for six weeks alternating with six weeks at home, in Lluesty. When money was provided for a new District General Hospital she had her acute beds there, a Psychogeriatric Unit was opened at the North Wales Hospital for Nervous Diseases and a Rehabilitation Unit and Day Hospital in Lluesty.

When the need for beds for Tuberculosis diminished with the advent of treatment with Streptomycin, she was able to use this spare facility in Llangwyfan for some of her patients from Lluesty and also 2 Wards were opened for Psychogeriatric patients.

In 1956, Dr Arnold had been advised to train in what was then the new speciality of Geriatrics, where there would be many openings including one in the Rhyl area. She spent 2 years working with the pioneer, Dr Marjorie Warren, at the West Middlesex Hospital, followed by the appointment as Senior Registrar at Whittington Hospital with Dr Exton-Smith. From Dr Warren she learnt about the importance of rehabilitation and with Dr Exton-Smith was involved in several research projects which included the value of hospital treatment in the elderly and the domiciliary assessment of social problems. Dr Exton-Smith was very keen on gadgets and believed in working as a team with

Nurses and Therapists. He helped to develop the Zimmer Frame which converted a ward of chair-bound patients into ambulant ones. He used engineers to observe the needs of patients on the wards and then worked out how these could be addressed. They showed that if patients were admitted at the start of their illness, very few were still in Hospital after 3 months. He had a good Physiotherapy Department and used occupational therapy. In the early 1960's Geriatric Departments for the active treatment of rehabilitation of the elderly sick were being developed throughout the country. When she became a Senior Registrar there were only four such posts in the United Kingdom; at Sunderland, Oxford, Scotland and the Whittington Hospital in London. The aim was to treat illness successfully. As degenerative disease was so common, complete cure was unusual and many patients had several disorders. They also aimed to improve the patients' ability to look after themselves and place them in surroundings suited to their capabilities and continued well-being. This work was co-ordinated with domiciliary and welfare services available to the elderly in the community.

Before she arrived in Rhyl she had drawn up her policy and stuck to it despite many difficulties. She was warmly welcomed by the two Consultant Physicians in Rhyl and also developed a good relationship with the General Practitioners. She was also fortunate to have excellent secretarial support who carried out the administrative work of the Department. Despite a constant battle to set standards, she initiated a first class service and before her first Consultant colleague was appointed, had been told that her Unit was of high standing in the country. She carried out assessments of Geriatric Units for the Health Advisory Department. She became a Consultant Assessor and was also involved in assessing Senior Registrar Training posts. She was a Member of several important medical committees and became Secretary of the Royal College of Physicians, Senior Registrar Training Committee for 7 years. Her great contribution was recognised in 1995 by the Award of the Presidents' Medal of the British Geriatric Society.

Dr Ellen S Emslie FRCP (Ed)
Consultant Dermatologist [1962-1992]

Dr Ellen Emslie was appointed Consultant Dermatologist by the Welsh Hospital Board and commenced her appointment on 1st January 1962. She had come to North Wales because her Consultant, when she was a Senior Registrar in Kings College Hospital London, was a Welshman from Anglesey and had advised her to apply despite being a non-Welsh Speaker. Dr Dorothy Lancaster, the previous Dermatologist, had died a year previously and the service had been kept going by General Practitioners – Dr Jack Lloyd Lewis in Bangor and Dr Ian Lynch in Rhyl, with help from a retired Consultant in the Conway Valley and Dr Aileen Hampton as Clinical Assistant. On her arrival in Rhyl, Dr Hampton had introduced herself to her and told her she was leaving to do other work, pursuing her career in Cytology.

Dr Emslie provided a dermatology service covering Bangor and Rhyl for the first six years of her appointment, until Dr Beer was appointed to Bangor and her job was split. She remained in Rhyl and also Llandudno and he provided a service to the West. She had clinics in the Royal Alexandra Hospital, Rhyl and four or five beds in HM Stanley Hospital, St Asaph; in Dr G Lloyd's Medical Ward.

At first she had no assistance from anyone who had had training in dermatology, but she enjoyed teaching and later five of her junior staff went on to become Consultant Dermatologists – including Richard Williams who is now the Senior Dermatologist in Glan Clwyd. One of her junior staff later became a Staff Grade Doctor in the Department and others

General Practitioners with an interest in Dermatology, who had had sessions in her department.

She was involved with the Postgraduate education of Doctors and became Secretary and later Chairman for three years of the Medical Postgraduate Board. She was Secretary and Chairman of the Hospital Medical Staff Committee; President of the North of England Dermatological Society and a long-standing Member of the Dowling Club, which was a Dermatology Travelling Club which gave her the opportunity to travel widely.

She visited Llangwyfan when invited to do so to see problem patients who might have skin eruptions due to drugs or following injections, or where the diagnosis was uncertain. Lupus Vulgaris (Tuberculosis of the skin) was not as common as in the past and could be controlled with INAH. She felt it would be easier for those who needed a skin biopsy to be referred to her clinic in Rhyl, rather than have this done in Llangwyfan.

When she arrived at Llangwyfan, Dr Biagi would escort her to see the patient and if more had been collected by Dr Gallagher, she always saw them all. A considerable number of patients had leg ulcers as Tuberculosis was more or less controlled towards the end.

Miss Catrin Williams FRCS (Ed) (1921-1998)
Consultant ENT Surgeon [1956-1986]

Miss Williams was appointed Consultant ENT Surgeon to Clwyd and Deeside Hospital Management Committee by the Welsh Regional Hospital Board in 1956, having her main base at St Asaph. She was a single-handed Consultant for almost 25 years and developed an ENT service for a wide geographical area. She had 3 operating lists a week, out-patient clinics and dealt with emergency work. She visited Llangwyfan when the need arose and carried out minor surgery there.

She enjoyed working with children and was an expert on guillotine Tonsillectomy – an operation now relegated to history. When major surgery such as Laryngectomy was carried out, this was done on a Saturday morning with the co-operation of the whole team, so as not to disrupt the other lists. She carried out over 100 Laryngectomies with good results though none in Llangwyfan. She was very supportive of these patients and their families and set up the first Laryngectomy Club in Wales, becoming their President.

She developed an interest in medical politics quite early, being a Member and Chairman of several committees in Clwyd. She was Chairman of East Denbigh and Flintshire Division of the BMA, Member of BMA Welsh Council and represented North Clwyd on the Annual Representative Meeting for many years.

She joined the Medical Women's Federation (MWF) shortly after coming to St Asaph and in 1973-74 became the Federation President, at that time the only Welsh woman to have held this honour. She was Career Adviser for medical women in North Wales from 1969 and helped married women with children to avail themselves of the retainer and retraining schemes. She was also very involved with the Medical Women's International Association, MWF Representative on the Women's National Commission and the United Nations Women's Advisory Committee.

She was elected a Member of the Executive Committee of the Women's National Commission three times, Co-Chairman of the National Commission 1981-83, was a Member of Committees chaired by Margaret Thatcher, Barbara Castle and Janet Young and was the MWF Member of an Ad-Hoc Working Group of the WNC chaired by Dame Ann Speakman who reported on "Women and the NHS".

She was a great traveller and travelled all over the world, attending conferences and post-conference tours. Following her retirement she continued her interest in those with hearing problems, becoming Chairman of the Welsh Council for the Deaf. She was an elected Member of Council and Executive Committee of the Royal National Institute for the Deaf and President of UK Ménière's Society.

Edward Lyons MB.ChB, DOMS, FRCOphth
Consultant Ophthalmologist [1954-1984]

Edward Lyons was a Consultant Ophthalmic Surgeon appointed by the Welsh Hospital Board and later by Clwyd Health Authority from 1954-1984. He founded the Ophthalmic Department at HM Stanley Hospital in 1954.

He had become interested in ophthalmology during his second appointment as House Surgeon in Sussex Eye Hospital, Brighton following which he obtained a 2 year appointment at Moorfields Eye Hospital, London. He was then conscripted into the RAMC to serve 2 years National Service. When he left the Army he returned to Moorfields as Chief Clinical Assistant part-time, became a part-time Senior Registrar at King Edward VIII Hospital, Windsor and a civilian eye specialist to the Cambridge Military Hospital, Aldershot so that his week was fully occupied. He had qualified from Leeds in 1944 and 10 years later he was appointed to this Consultant post where he remained for the rest of his professional career.

In school and university he had been a good sportsman and was nominated on to the Students Representative Council, eventually becoming Chairman. He was elected President in 1942-1943 and had participated in Rag Revues as a student to raise funds for charity.

After gaining his Consultant appointment his interest in medical administration and the political sphere continued from being Chairman of the Hospital Medical Staff Committee, to representing hospital medical staff from Clwyd and Deeside at the Medical Advisory Committee to the Welsh Hospital Board, Clwyd Local Medical Committee and Clwyd Family Practitioner Committee, and he was a member of the Secretary of State for Wales Steering Committee on Reorganisation of the NHS 1971-1972.

He was a great supporter of the BMA and was Chairman of the Welsh Committee for Hospital Medical Services 1972-1975; a Member of the Welsh Council and Member of the Central Council (representing hospital doctors in Wales) 1970-1976.

He joined the Rotary Club of Abergele in 1972 becoming President in 1982. He was a Founder Member of Llanddulas Youth Club Management Committee and is now a Life President and Vice-President of the Welsh Association of Youth Clubs. His interests involve ornithology and natural history and he is a supporter and past Chairman of the Friends of the North Wales Medical Aid to Tamil Nadu.

Edward Lyons visited Llangwyfan monthly for several years to examine patients who needed an ophthalmic opinion following his appointment in 1954. He carried out refractions with a view to ordering glasses if necessary on those patients selected by Dr Biagi. Occasionally he gave an opinion on the fundus of an eye and advice on minor eye conditions. He rarely visited a ward since a room was made available for his 'mini clinic'. He could not recall carrying out any surgery although he might have carried out an incision and curettage of a meibomian cyst.

Dr Muriel Margaret McLean MD, FRCP (Ed), DCH
[1920-1991]
Consultant Paediatrician [1957-1980]

Dr McLean, daughter of the Reverend David W McLean, a Minister in the Presbyterian Church of Scotland, was born on the 26th May 1920 in Macduff Town. Her father moved to Gamrie when she was 3 years old and remained there until his death in 1932, when her mother with her family of five children moved to Banff.

Muriel was the fourth of five children, the eldest being Vida, who became a teacher. Her sister Irene, a Dentist who was the third child had moved to live in America when she married and had one son who became a Dentist. She had one brother, Ian, who died before her mother and another, David, the youngest, who studied Dentistry and practised in Cheshire.

Muriel went to school in Banff Academy and then to University to study medicine which she had always wanted to do, in Aberdeen, qualifying in 1942.

She worked in the Sick Children's Hospital in Glasgow for a short time and as a General Practitioner in Scotland before joining the RAMC in 1944 and being deployed to India which she enjoyed, working in Abbottabad, Pakistan and Rawalpindi. She was discharged in 1947 and continued her postgraduate training in Aberdeen as a Registrar and Senior Registrar. She gained the Diploma in Child Health in 1948, MRCP (Ed) 1951, MD 1955 and FRCP in 1959.

She came to Rhyl in 1957 having had a family holiday in Llanfairfechan in 1955 and liked the area. Her post entailed being responsible for the care of sick children in the Children's Ward in the Royal Alexandra Hospital, Rhyl; a unit of 18 acute medical beds and cots; and also the care of the newborn in the Obstetric Unit, having 54 cots in HM Stanley Hospital, St Asaph 7 miles away. She held clinics and provided cover when needed in other hospitals in the area including Llangwyfan, where as a Scot she would have been particularly welcomed by the Biagi's, and attended the hospital parties.

She had met Anne Sutherland in Aberdeen and they became friends and Anne joined her in Rhyl in 1963 where they worked well together until her retirement. Dr McLean was the sole Consultant in her speciality until she was joined by Dr A J

Williams in 1977 and by Dr T Youlle in 1980.

When she first arrived in Rhyl she shared a houseman with Dr Geoffrey Lloyd who had beds on the same floor and was a General Physician with an interest in Neurology: she had to cope with emergencies at night and would return home in the morning for a shower and breakfast before returning to work, but she never complained. Until Anne Sutherland joined her, Dr Gerald Roberts of Wrexham would cover her work when she took a holiday. She was particularly firm with Ivor Lewis who wanted to keep children on the Surgical Ward, insisting that they be nursed instead on the Children's Ward.

She was completely dedicated to the children who were under her care and provided a first class service under very trying conditions. Towards the end she had health problems but on retirement joined the Citizens Advice Bureau in Prestatyn, becoming its Chairman. When I became Secretary of the Hospital Medical Staff Committee she was my first Chairman and I found her very easy and supportive to work with, possessing a very good intellect and humour. She became very involved in postgraduate education in Rhyl and established the Library, becoming the Honorary Librarian, before Mr John Bladen, the first professional Librarian was appointed. She was also responsible for choosing all the furnishings and curtains for the new postgraduate Centre in the Royal Alexandra Hospital, Rhyl having excellent administrative support from Mrs Hughes.

Her death was sudden after taking her dogs for a walk. She was unmarried, but her life is remembered with gratitude by the countless children who benefited from her care.

Dr Tim Alban Lloyd MC, BCh, FRCPath (1916-1983)
First Consultant Pathologist [1951-1981]

John Timothy Alban Lloyd was born on the 30th July 1916 in Nottingham of Welsh parents, his father being from Aberdaron and his mother from Caernarfon. His father was a Prison Chaplain at Nottingham, Dartmoor and Strangeways, Manchester. His grandfather had been Rector of Aberdaron (1907-1910) and his brother became Rector of Bala and Pentrefoelas. Tim's mother's father was Mayor of Caernarfon for three years (1875/6/7). He was a Wine Merchant in the town.

Tim was educated in Rossall School and the University of Manchester. After one house appointment he was called up and for the rest of the war served in the RAMC mainly as Medical Officer to an Infantry Battalion. He served with the 8th Army through the North African Campaign then in Italy and in the Normandy Landings. He was awarded the Military Cross for gallantry in the field. He had deliberately driven into an enemy-held village accompanied by his Sergeant and jeep driver to evacuate a seriously wounded British Officer. The German Commander gave his consent but insisted a captured German Officer be freed in exchange. When Tim saw the wounded officer he recognised him as an old fellow student from Manchester. He dressed his wounds, placed him in the jeep and he was returned, but later died. Tim had to wait three hours to be freed following the return of the German Officer. He was at El Alamein and in the first hour of the D-Day Landings at Arromanche where he set up a Field Hospital in a Church.

On his return to Manchester he decided to specialise in Pathology and worked in Manchester Royal Infirmary and Hope Hospital, Salford. He gained the Diploma in Pathology in 1951, the year he gained his appointment as the First Consultant Pathologist appointed to North Clwyd where he developed a service from a base in the Royal Alexandra Hospital, Rhyl. At first his unit was in a small converted kitchen in the basement, then to larger premises in a converted laundry next-door to a coal dump and boiler house. He provided a service to over 14 hospitals in the area including Llangwyfan and from a small staff of a Secretary and two Technicians his Department grew and specialised. In 1980 he was able to lead it into the new District General Hospital which had a large well equipped clinical Laboratory and whose museum is now dedicated and named after him. Sarah Davies (née Roberts) was a Trainee Technician in the Royal Alexandra Hospital and told me that she remembered specimens coming from Llangwyfan though she was never sent there. Tim, though, travelled extensively and in all weathers to visit all the hospitals, and with John Richards set up the Laboratory in Llangwyfan in the early 1950's.

He had been appointed a General Clinical Pathologist but later became interested in haematology and histopathology, especially in the care of the elderly. He became a Founder Fellow of the Royal College of Pathologists in 1963 and retired in 1981. However, after a short illness he died on the 4th May 1983.

He was a member of many committees, working parties, planning groups and at one time was a member of Clwyd Health Authority, the Clwyd Medical Committee and the Welsh Advisory Committee in Pathology. He was President of the Cambrian Branch of Association of Clinical Pathologists, Chairman of West Denbighshire and Flint Division of the BMA and Tutor to Manchester Undergraduates in Rhyl.

A man of integrity whose opinions were sought and a father figure to many, especially those in his Department, he was one of the 'wise men' whose concern for his staff led to their devotion and loyalty. In retirement he played golf and was an active Freemason. His wife, Jean, was a former Nurse and they had four children. Trish is a Nurse, specialising in children with cleft palates and was awarded an MBE for services to nursing. Sue became a Teacher and works with young criminals. Peter owns a loft conversion company and Edward is the Managing Director of Swayne Johnson Solicitors.

Dr Charles Hilton Jones MD, FRC Path
Consultant Pathologist in Rhyl [1962-1989]

Charles qualified in Liverpool in 1948 and after house jobs carried out his military service in the Army. He carried out an investigation into BCG vaccination, which I described in my first book on Llangwyfan, on Army Personnel, which was successful and resulted in helping to bring about massive vaccinations of all children for the next 50 years. On demobilisation he returned to Liverpool to work in Alder Hey Children's Hospital and then returned to the University as a Lecturer in Pathology until his appointment as Consultant Pathologist to Clwyd and Deeside HMC.

He wrote an article to a Medical Journal on his experience of being a Medical Student in Liverpool in war-time and attended a conference in London in 1947 as the representative from Liverpool Medical School, to meet the Right Honourable Aneurin Bevan MP. He remembers this occasion as a remarkable performance when Bevan recommended to them that the National Health Service should start the following year. A room had been booked for him to stay on the Saturday night in the London Hospital, which he had to find late that night, and remembers it as a frightening experience when he got lost in the East End.

He used to attend Clinical-Pathological Conferences in Llangwyfan in the 1960's and was one of the Founders and mainstays of Postgraduate Education as well as Undergraduate Education in Rhyl. There had not been anything like it before the NHS and he became Secretary of the Postgraduate Board and later the Chairman, maintaining his interest in it afterwards and being pleased that it had been so successful. He enjoyed teaching and supporting the young undergraduates who came to Rhyl from Liverpool.

Dr Rodney Irwin Green MD, DMRD [1924-2002]
Consultant Radiologist in Rhyl [1958-1984]

The X-ray Department in Rhyl had been set up by Dr Pierce Williams the first Consultant Radiologist appointed by the Welsh Regional Hospital Board to oversee services in Rhyl and Colwyn Bay. Dr Pierce Williams had previously been a General Practitioner in Colwyn Bay and had developed an interest in Radiology. When Dr Green was appointed in 1958, Dr Pierce Williams decided to have Colwyn Bay as his Headquarters with Dr Green looking after Rhyl and developing the service in the Royal Alexandra Hospital. Although he worked well with Dr Pierce Williams, their personalities did not compliment each other and there were divisions of opinion.

Dr Green was born in Liverpool, attended Liverpool College School and proceeded to Liverpool University where he qualified M.B. B.Ch in 1947. He was the younger of two brothers, his brother Norman being a Schoolmaster before becoming a Priest and then a Lawyer. He was six years older than Rodney and had been in the Army in India undertaking his National Service.

Rodney did all his training in hospitals in the Liverpool Region such as the Royal Northern, Royal Southern and Royal Infirmary and attended the Liverpool Radiology Course where during his last year he was joined by Dr Gordon Row and the two became life-long great friends. Rodney obtained an MD in 1957 from the University of Liverpool for a Thesis on the Radiological Appearance of the Soft Palate and Nasopharynx following treatment of Cleft Palate with special reference to Palato – Pharyngeal analysis and speech results.

Later in 1965 Dr Gordon Row joined him in Rhyl and they

created a modern department and service for the scattered hospitals of North Clwyd, including Llangwyfan. They were on friendly terms with Dr Biagi and would visit Llangwyfan in turn to read the X-rays until at the end all the X-rays were sent to Rhyl for reporting. They had a good rapport with all grades of staff and departments, which made working conditions smooth and Rodney also had a good sense of humour, was proactive, worked hard and did all the extra work needed. Gordon was the perfect foil and they complemented each other perfectly.

Rodney had been an asthmatic since childhood and would give himself adrenaline injections, had been in hospital with Pulmonary Tuberculosis and was very deaf. All these disabilities did not prevent him from partaking in a full life.

He had become interested in music through having a job as an usher in the Philharmonic Hall when he was a student and developed this interest throughout his life becoming Chairman of Rhyl Music Club. Always keen on sport such as cricket and hockey in school, he later became very keen on golf playing it twice a week. He was a supporter of the cricket match between St Asaph and Rhyl Hospitals and represented either as needs demanded, batting regularly in the early years of this friendly contest.

Due to eye problems he had to give up driving in the last few years and he bought an electric bicycle, but discovered that that was not safe to ride in traffic on country lanes as the tyres could get slashed by the edge of the road.

He became interested in paintings through his mother, with whom he lived until his marriage. His mother bought paintings and then sold them at a profit to make money; a gift she shared with Rodney and they visited exhibitions, dealers and antique fairs together. He collected old English water colours but after his death his widow sold them as they were becoming an encumbrance.

He married Jean, a Surgeon, in 1958 and they had four

children. Helen, the eldest, became an IT specialist and lives in Mansfield; Richard is a Motor Mechanic living in Gellifor and is at hand to support her; Sally is a General Practitioner in Oxford and has four children and Jeremy the youngest became a Radiologist. Despite his deafness Rodney had chaired several committees such as the Hospital Medical Staff Committee and the Clwyd Medical Committee and had been a Member of the Welsh Medical Committee at the same time as Dr John Lynch with whom he often travelled to meetings. After retiring at 60 years of age, he continued undertaking locums for another 10 years until the age of 70.

Dr Herbert Gordon Row DMRD [1929-2003]
Consultant Radiologist, Rhyl [C.1960's-1995]

Gordon Row was born in Appleby in 1929, the son of a Bank Manager. He was educated at Appleby Grammar School before proceeding to study medicine in Liverpool where he qualified in 1952. He did the Radiology Course in Liverpool, under Dr Percy Whittaker, Consultant Radiologist, where he met Rodney Green and they became life-long good friends. He did his Army Service in Transkei, Kenya where he met and married Rosemary, the daughter of a Farmer who loved the outdoor life. They had three children; Sally who is a General Practitioner in Otley, Caroline an Accountant and a son who is a Dentist, David.

Gordon joined Rodney in the Department in Rhyl and they worked well together for the rest of their lives, until Rodney retired. Between them they created a stress-free Department. They shared the work visiting in turn Holywell, Abergele, Llangwyfan, the Royal Alexandra and War Memorial Hospitals, Rhyl, and HM Stanley Hospital. Later on, due to the increased work, they cut the travelling and films taken for reporting were sent to Rhyl. He semi-retired in 1992 then did locums until 1995.

He was a good committee person and became the Consultants' Medical Representative on the Health Authority, a job he found stressful dealing with "egos". He was a good negotiator and mediator, very easy to deal with and get on with. He died on the 7th January 2003 aged 73 years.

Mr Owen Daniel MS, FRCS
Consultant Surgeon, Rhyl [1960-1982]

Owen Daniel was appointed Consultant Surgeon in Rhyl following the retirement of Mr Ivor Lewis. He had previously been a Senior Lecturer in Surgery in Sheffield and Honorary Consultant Surgeon to the United Sheffield Hospitals.

Born in Breconshire he had his medical education in University College Hospital Medical School, London, having won scholarships to study there and where he gained the Liston Gold Medal in Clinical Surgery in 1941. He had been a Surgeon Lieutenant, RNVR(T) from 1945 to 1947 and his love of the sea never left him. He enjoyed the solitude of yachting off the North Wales coast as a means of relaxing after busy days in Rhyl. He also went on longer trips with his brother, Sir Goronwy Daniel, to Ireland and with his sons Rhodri and Ivor to Brittany, Scotland and the Isle of Man.

He had worked in the Postgraduate Medical School in Hammersmith for eight years where he had carried out research and for three years of this time he had worked in Centres of Excellence in the United States, in John Hopkins Hospital School, Baltimore and Cornell University Medical School, New York.

He was twice Hunterian Professor, Royal College of Surgeons of England in 1960 and 1970, and he was given a grant from the Welsh Scheme for Locally Organised Clinical Research, from 1960-1979 from which his junior staff benefited. He became

Royal Party outside Children's Block – July 16th, 1920.
Sir Robert Jones (First Consultant Orthopaedic Surgeon appointed to WNMA), Lord David Davies, Llandinam (President WNMA), HRH Princess Mary, HRH King George V, Sir D W Evans (Sec. WNMA), Miss Nesta Davies, Sir D S Davies, MP, Denbigh (who bequethed Llangwyfan to the Welsh National Memorial Association). Behind the Princess' right shoulder is Dr Evans, Medical Superintendent and behind the King's right shoulder is Taliesin Rees, Architect of the Sanatorium

Staff group outside Administrative Block – 1952.
Dr Biagi is sitting in the middle of the front row with Miss Morrison, Matron on his right and Miss Salt,
Hospital Administrator on his left, Dr Gallagher on her left

Aerial veiw of Llangwyfan

Peter Wilson on his motor-bike

Staff Nurse Peter Wilson

British Tuberculosis Association Badge
belonging to Peter Wilson

Peter Wilson BTA Certificate

Reg. No. PS4107

This is to Certify that

Peter L Wilson

has completed a Term of training at

Llangwyfan Hospital

has attended the Courses of Lectures,
received the Practical Instruction
prescribed and has passed the Written
and Oral Examinations of the British
Tuberculosis Association in the Nursing
of Cases of Pulmonary Tuberculosis.

President - British Tuberculosis Association

Chairman Examination Committee

K.R.Stone

Hon. Secretary

Date *November 1958*

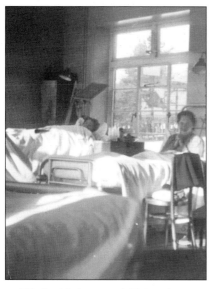

'I' in bed in her ward. Note mirror above the bed to assist reading and eating

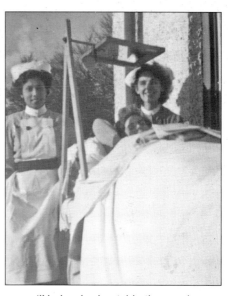

'I' in her bed outside the ward with Sister Griffiths and Nurse

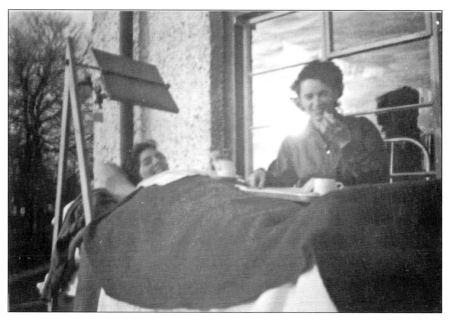

'I' outside in bed showing extra covering on the bed and tray of food and drink

A card from Nansi Richards to 'I's mother. Nansi Richards came from a farm the other side of the mountain from where 'I' lived outside Bala. She was the star harpist of her day and was a family friend. This is one of 'I's treasures.

The reverse side of the card, when she was on tour in the USA.

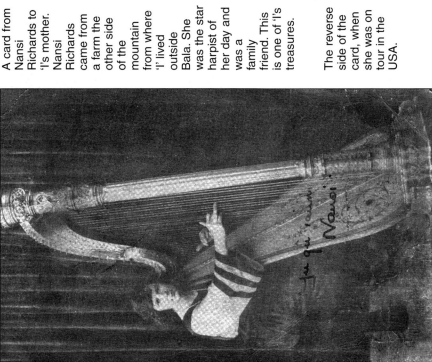

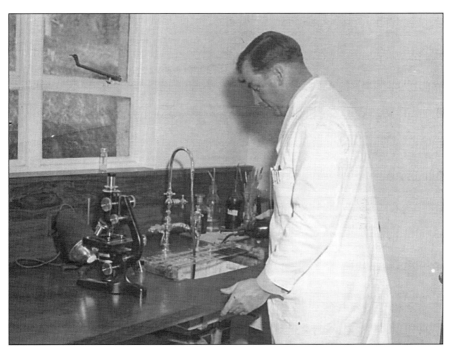

John Richards - Lab Technician

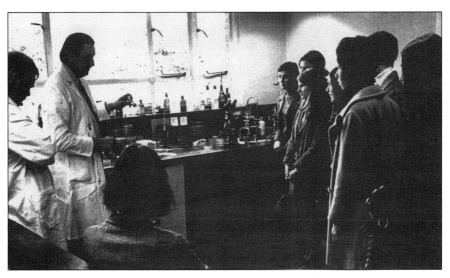

Brian Cowlishaw demonstrating equipment to girls from Howell's School Denbigh in Pulmonary Lab

Kate Williams, Sister Tutor with Matron – Miss B Morris

On the bus to Denbigh Moors. *Front right:* Sister Penn (Hut A) and Anwen Jones behind her. They were taking male patients for an outing

Denbigh Moors. Patients in front. Anwen Jones and Agnes Hill at back

Agnes Hill
Kate Williams
(Senior Tutor)
and Anwen Jones

Whole group on Denbigh Moors.
Front row: Matron Morris (wearing white hat), to the right and behind Matron – Miss Coombs

Above:
Llangwyfan 1954 –
Block 9
Left to right:
Emily (Denbigh),
Sr Freda Jones
(Hendrerwydd),
Megan Evans
(Capel Curig),
Dr Novak,
Anwen Jones,
Dr Munier.
Sitting: Bob Deed,
Enid Williams

Nurses – 1950s.
Megan Evans (Capel
Curig),
Mair Davies
(Denbigh),
Gwyneth Jones
(Llanfyllin),
Agnes Hill (Llŷn),
Anwen Jones
(Derwen).

Reunion (50 years) of Student Nurses (1953) in Llangwyfan,
taken in Denbigh.
Maria Garlip (Germany), Megan Evans (Capel Curig), Carmel Griffiths (Anglesey),
Anwen Jones (Derwen), Agnes Hill (Pwllheli) Cara

Gwyn Pierce Williams as a patient.
Gwyn and his mother

Gwyn in front of pond

Gwyn in back row 2nd from right

Gwyn 2nd
from right on
back row with
X above head

Children 1967 in Fancy Dress
From left to right: John Ivor Jones, Stephen Latham, Dawn Hough,
Stephen Pierce, Gareth Wynn Jones. *Front:* Heather Roberts

Llangwyfan 1967

Outside Block 7
–1967

Summer Fete – Mrs K. W. Parry (Sec.), Mrs. Claudia Davies (Chair),
Mrs Ffoulkes (opened Fete), Carol Downes (patient), Matron Morris
– Carol presenting Mrs Ffoulkes with flowers

Staff Fancy Dress – 1968.
From left back: Robert Holmes, Megan Williams,
Anne Davies, Joan Potts, Dr Sahola, Sister Waine (at end).
Front left: Annie Jones, Mrs Brown, Mr Hughes (Headmaster)

1968 Children in front of Block: *Back row left to right:* Joan Potts (N/Aux.),
Ian Williams, Stephen Crewe (black blazer), Ifor Downes, Sr Waine.
Irene Downes, Carol Downes, Pearl Downes, David, John Jones, Llawenna
Downes, John Joey Stamp, Jacqueline Hughes, Llewelyn Gary Griffiths, Alwena,
Kathy – NOTE: 5 children from one family

Carol Downes holding flowers in Summer Fete. Behind her right shoulder – David Jones, Hospital Secretary

Margaret Williams (Aux Nurse) with patient

Wyn with family – going home

1972 – Llangwyfan Queen crowning – Llandyrnog Queen in attendance

2007 – Twins with Book each. Great-grandchildren of Will and Nellie Jones. Rachel holding the book, Emma about to start. Mr W. T. Jones was Head Gardener and died in 1943

1969 – Llangwyfan Queen crowning – Llandyrnog Queen in attendance.
Carys Jones (Queen), *back left:* Janet Lloyd,
Jacqueline Hughes (white dress)

Sister Alice Jones – a Sister in Llangwyfan in 1950s.
The background is not Llangwyfan

Er Serchog Goffadwriaeth

AM

ALICE

merch annwyl i Mr. a Mrs. J. E. Jones

PEN-Y-BRYN, COED ACCAS, Ger DINBYCH

a chwaer hoffus i Betty, Robert David ac Edwin

Hunodd yn dawel Ebrill 10, 1957

YN 31 MLWYDD OED

Rhoddwyd ei gweddillion i orffwys ym Mynwent y Groes, prynhawn Sadwrn, Ebrill 13, 1957.

"Hyn a allodd hon, hi a'i gwnaeth"

Funeral Service – Alice Jones

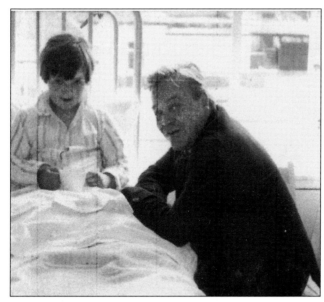

Alwena Jones with Patrick Wymark (actor). In 2008 Alwena told me that her illness had made her realise that health was the most important thing in life and it also made her more determined

Back row, left to right: N/Aux Blodwen Jones, Ivor Downes, John Islwyn Jones, Llewelyn Hughes, Patrick Wymark (actor on a visit), Matron Morris, Staff Nurse holding Sylvia Downes (baby), Staff Nurse Tinseley holding Joey Stamp.
Second row: John Stamp, Paul Andrews, Kathy Edwards, Carol Downes, Jacky Hughes, Llawenna Jones, Irene Downes

Sister Waine at her desk

Mr Hugh Reid and hospital staff

Dr E Clifford Jones

Kellett Jones
(dentist) with
Margaret Coop
his wife
(radiographer)

Dr Green - Consultant Radiologist

In March 1982 the title of Penrose May Teacher was conferred on Mr Owen Daniel, MS, FRCS by the President of the Royal College of Surgeons of England, Sir Allan Parks, on his retirement as Advisor on the training of Surgeons for North Wales in recognition of his outstanding contribution to teaching and training for many years

Dr David Rowlands (centre front) and his daughter, Kate, holding the MBE she received for her work in Afghanistan

Members Clwyd and Deeside HMC – 1948.
Back row left to right: Mr A. D. H. Pennant, Mr. E. K. H. Turnor, Dr Ifor Davies (GP), William Roberts (Group Sec. 1948-1962), H. Clifford Robinson (Dental Surgeon), D. I. Currie (Surgeon), A. H. Holmes (GP Obstetician).
Front row: Cllr J. H. Williams, Ald. Mrs C. Lloyd (JP), Ald. G. O. Williams (NBE, JP – Vice-chair 1948-1960), Dr Huw T. Edwards (JP – Chairman 1948-1967), Mrs G. M. Heaton (CBE – Vice-chairman 1960-1964), Mrs D. Waterhouse

Miss Salt Leaving Party

Standing: Iorwerth Jones, Thomas Henry Evans, Bert Cray, Doris Roberts, Mrs Dickens, Helen Roberts, Bill Savage

Seated: William Roberts, C & D HMC Secretary), Miss Salt, Dr Biagi, Matron Morris

The medical staff checking x-rays – late 1950s.
Left to right: ?, ?, Dr Penrhyn Jones, Dr Gallagher, Dr Mayer, Dr Novak,
Dr Biagi

Staff and patients in ward – c. late 1950

Dr Mayer leaving Llangwyfan – 1950s.
Dr Bapat, ?, Dr Munro, Mr G Fielding (Brisbane), Dr Biagi, Dr Mayer, ?,
Matron Morris, ?.

Pharmacy – Gertie Hughes (Dispenser) with Sr Humphreys

Autoclaves and Sterilizers – 1955

Laundry

CLWYD AND DEESIDE HOSPITAL MANAGEMENT COMMITTEE

Llangwyfan Hospital

Dedication of
Hospital Chapel

Dedication of the Hospital Chapel

By THE LORD BISHOP OF ST. ASAPH (The Right Reverend D. D. Bartlett)

THE REVEREND ELFYN ELLIS and

FATHER J. WEDLAKE

MONDAY, 10th APRIL, 1967

Chapel inside

Cllr Huw T Edwards - Chairman Clwyd
and Deeside HMC

Ald G O Williams MBE JP
Vice-Chairman

Blodwen Morris
and patient in
Garden of
Remembrance

Surgical Tutor to the Royal College of Surgeons of England, and also its Regional Surgical Adviser for North Wales. He was also the author of 45 articles in various scientific journals.

His first Hunterian Lecture was on "Total Cystectomy and Uretro-Colic Anastomosis". His second on "The Value of Radiomanometry in Bile Duct Surgery" was carried out while he was working in Rhyl. On his retirement he was honoured with an Honorary Professorship by the College for his postgraduate tutorial work with young surgeons. He had succeeded in establishing an Anatomy Centre in Rhyl associated with the Anatomy Department and Professorial Unit of the University of Liverpool so that junior medical staff could undertake anatomical dissection of body parts locally.

Following his retirement he undertook locum work for Consultant Surgeons in Rhyl and Wrexham for five years, and was also a Member of a Tribunal Board in South Wales considering Disability Benefit for almost ten years.

He had in 1974, following the successful transfer of surgical services from Rhyl to Llangwyfan, suggested that Llangwyfan had the potential to be used to house a surgical unit for the third surgeon appointed to Rhyl, but instead a convalescent unit was created there.

He had been honoured by the National Eisteddfod of Wales with a White Robe, was interested in Welsh history, poetry and literature. He had in the first ten years of his retirement enjoyed farming in Carmarthenshire breeding sheep and Welsh Black Cattle and taking an active part during the lambing season.

His wife, Rhianydd, was a National Eisteddfod Soprano winner and trained in the Guildhall School of Music. They had three sons, the eldest Rhodri becoming a Consultant Ophthalmologist in Moorfields Hospital, Ivor having a career in social work and education with Gloucester County Council, and Huw is President of the Platinum Guild International of America.

O M Jonathan FRCS, MRCS, LRCP, MBBS
Consultant Surgeon (Clwyd Health Authority) – Rhyl
[1961-1983]

Owen Morris Jonathan's forbears were farmers and businessmen in Anglesey and Gwynedd. He was born in Anglesey during the first world war. His father who held commissioned rank with the Royal Welsh Fusiliers with the Machine Gun Corps was on active service in France at the time, but was given compassionate leave to come back to Anglesey for his birth. He was brought up in Towyn, Merioneth and after leaving school took his 1st MB in the University College of Wales, Aberystwyth before proceeding to Guy's Hospital Medical School, University of London for his medical training. After graduating and house jobs he joined the Royal Army Medical Corps, was commissioned 1943-1946, and saw active service in Burma, French Indo-China and the Dutch East Indies.

On discharge he worked in the Postgraduate Medical School of London and Lambeth Hospital before moving to Wrexham and Cardiff. He spent time as a Clinical Instructor in Surgery in Wisconsin USA and also worked in St Peters Hospital in London for Genitourinary Disease and St Mark's Hospital for Diseases of the Colon and Rectum. He was appointed Consultant Surgeon to Merthyr and then after two years came to Rhyl in 1961. During the first 12 years of this appointment he was one of two surgeons involved in the development and expansion of the surgical work in the Clwyd North District. This was a heavy workload and a third surgeon was appointed in 1975. He was also involved in postgraduate teaching at undergraduate and postgraduate level. One of his publications was on Massive Tuberculose Pyonephrosis complicating Pregnancy. He also carried out an epidemiological and surgical review of Hydatid Disease in North Wales which was published in the British Medical Journal.

Prior to the opening of Glan Clwyd Hospital the three

surgeons who were mainly based at the Royal Alexandra Hospital in Rhyl often visited both Llangwyfan and Abergele Hospitals to see patients who had developed surgical problems, so were quite familiar with both hospitals. During one period of several months whilst renovation work in the theatre and wards of the Alexandra Hospital was carried out; the whole surgical staff medical and nursing was transferred to Llangwyfan. Although there were difficulties due to the absence of a lift at Llangwyfan, the experience was both rewarding and enjoyable mainly due to the enthusiastic support of Dr Biagi and his staff, as well as the invigorating effect of driving through beautiful countryside on the way to work!

After the surgical unit had returned to Rhyl, a new convalescent unit was established at Llangwyfan which necessitated supervision by the medical staff of both hospitals. The unit remained there until Glan Clwyd was opened and resulted in a marked improvement in the bed occupancy and turnover of surgical patients as well as closer contact between the visiting and resident staff of both hospitals.

After he retired he was appointed by the British Council as Visiting Professor of Surgery to the University of Kenya, Nairobi for 6 months. Later, for 3 months, he was Visiting Surgeon and Lecturer in Surgery to the Christian Medical College, Ludhiana, and to other areas of India. In 1987 he returned to Glan Clwyd as Consultant Surgeon for 12 months. For the 8 years following he was a Member of the Medical Appeal Tribunal for Wales and Liverpool. Despite his workload he did not find it stressful but enjoyed the challenge of operating in different fields and getting good results and training the many young doctors who came from different parts of the world to work in Rhyl – from Australia, Assam, Tasmania and Canada.

He enjoyed walking and in his late seventies he joined a group of colleagues in a geriatric odyssey which involved walking the 176 miles of Offa's Dyke. His colleagues dropped off one by one, which left him to walk the second half of the journey on his own. It was necessary to succeed because he had been sponsored, and was greatly aided by his military son-in-law who advised the daily use of surgical spirit for his feet to prevent blisters. The ten day walk raised £1,500 for charity.

His wife, Lowri came from a sea-faring family and she served in the Navy as a WREN Officer for five years during the war. She died at the time of his retirement and he has a devoted family of three children and eight grandchildren. Unfortunately, one of whom was tragically killed in 2008. His daughter Ann trained as a Nurse at St Thomas' Hospital, Owen the elder son is a Lawyer in London and David trained at Guy's Hospital Medical School like his father and is a surgeon.

Edward Wood FRCS [1937-2006]
Consultant Surgeon – Rhyl

He qualified from Birmingham in 1961 and after house jobs in Hereford and Birmingham he trained as a General and Vascular Surgeon in Glasgow and was appointed the third surgeon with an interest in vascular surgery to the Rhyl group of hospitals in North Wales. He had convalescent beds at Llangwyfan. Unfortunately Mr Wood retired aged 52 years on ill-health and died in 2006 aged 69 years.

Stewart Hunter, MRCOG
Consultant Obstetrician and Gynaecologist,
HM Stanley Hospital, St Asaph [1967-1970]

Mr Stewart Hunter was only in the area for three years. He had come from South Africa and left to go to Canada, so was a nomad and remembered as rather a flamboyant character. He operated in St Asaph and had convalescent beds in Llangwyfan. He carried out a ward round in Llangwyfan once a week. His anaesthetic colleague in St Asaph was Dr John Lynch.

A letter from Dr Biagi to the Right Honourable Geraint Morgan MP gives some clarification on why he was only in the area a short time. At one time he wished to have beds in Llangwyfan to carry out Gynaecological Surgery because of bed problems in St Asaph, but this was sat on immediately and indirectly because of this he left the area in the early 1970's.

Dr Ken Hardy FRCA
Consultant Anaesthetist – Bangor [1962-1985]

Dr Hardy was a Consultant Anaesthetist in Bangor from 1962 – 1985. Born in Manchester he was a Foundation Scholar in Manchester Grammar School, one of the country's top schools, and in 1940 evacuated to Bala where he attended Bala Grammar School. He trained in Liverpool but did no anaesthetic jobs in England.

After house jobs in London he was Senior Medical Officer on a troopship, taking troops to Korea 1952 – 1954. At this time, a lot of Irish Doctors were coming over to the United Kingdom to work, entering General Practice, and it was difficult for home graduates to get into Practice. Consequently, when he was discharged he decided to try anaesthetics.

He was appointed Senior House Officer, then Registrar in Bangor from where he got a similar post in Cardiff followed by a Senior Registrar appointment there. During his time in Cardiff he went to Boston Massachusetts as a Senior Registrar Lecturer, as Professor W W Mushin, Professor of Anaesthesia in the Welsh National School of Medicine liked his Senior Registrars to have experience of working in the United States of America.

He was then appointed to Bangor in 1962 where he remained

and where one of his first goals was to learn Welsh. His wife, Bethan, daughter of a well known Preacher, was a big help to him in this regard and in bringing up their Welsh speaking family. They have had 10 grandchildren; one of whom was tragically killed in 2007 whilst studying as a student in Liverpool.

Dr Hardy was elected President of the British and Irish Intractable Pain Society, and during this time visited and worked in the Pain Clinic in Adelaide, South Australia, where Professor Mike Cousins was the Professor of Anaesthesia. He started one of the first pain clinics in this country and at one time was the Postgraduate Organiser and Librarian in Bangor. He is a Past President of the Society of Anaesthetists of Wales and Cymdeithas Poen Cymru (Wales Pain Society). He was honoured to be appointed Member of the Gorsedd of the National Eisteddfod, gaining the White Robe. He was the Founder of the Gwynedd Branch of the Samaritans.

Before Ysbyty Gwynedd opened he was appointed Medical Consultant Liaison Officer to the Commissioning Team for what he thought was 2 years, but turned out to be a six year period. He told me that "it was a most enjoyable experience and it taught him a lot".

At the time he started in Llangwyfan Mr Hugh Reid had just finished operating there and Mr R Doyle, Genitourinary Surgeon had started. Mr Doyle had felt he owed a debt to Llangwyfan as he had been offered work there before he got established. Even at that time Dr Hardy was aware of plans to try and close Llangwyfan and of Dr Biagi's determination to keep it open.

He went there for 2-3 years, driving over the Denbigh Moors which made it a very happy visit driving through lovely scenery. He went on a Monday, occasionally the list being held in the evening to accommodate Mr Doyle. He anaesthetised occasionally for an ENT list or for Dr Biagi to do Bronchoscopies.

Dr David Rowlands MB. BCh, DA, FRCA
Consultant Anaesthetist – Llandudno [1953-1985]

Dr Rowlands wrote:

"I visited Llangwyfan several times in the mid 1930s. The Medical Superintendent, Dr Fenwick Jones ("Uncle Dai") was a friend of my father's and it was at his suggestion that I considered Medicine as a career.

The Hospital had recently acquired an adjoining estate (Vron Yw); most of its attractive two-storied house had become the Medical Superintendent's Residence, with a small part separated for the use of one of the hospital engineers.

At that time the treatment for tuberculosis seemed to be bed rest and good food, with graduated exercises and increasing work in the farms and gardens under medical supervision as the patient's condition improved.

The hospital had its own electricity generating plant, the exhaust steam from which provided hot water for the laundry.

When I became a consultant in 1953 I visited Llangwyfan occasionally, and later took over Dr Harry Edwards' Friday morning session. I gained considerable kudos in my family as I anaesthetised for Mr Howell Hughes on more than one occasion, so must be reasonably competent! I always found Llangwyfan to be a friendly place to work.

I was not an enthusiast for suxamethonium (a short acting muscle relaxant), partly because of the post-anaesthetic aches and pains, but mainly for the long action of the drug occasionally necessitating ventilating the patient for several hours until its effect wore off. This could cause inconvenience if I had finished the list at Llangwyfan at 11:00 am and was due in Bangor for another list at 2:00 pm but couldn't leave until the patient had recovered.

One Sunday morning I was asked if I would mind coming over in case an anaesthetic was required for a possible appendicectomy on the Deputy Medical Superintendent's child. Mr Hugh Reid was on his way from Liverpool to see the patient, and it was felt tactless to ask Nancie to anaesthetise, as Ivor had not been invited to operate!

It was decided that no operation was required. I stayed for lunch, after which the Medical Superintendent's wife washed the dishes, which were dried by the Medical Superintendent and myself, a marked contrast to prewar when there had been a cook and one or two maids in uniform supplied by the hospital."

Dr Pat Barry FRCA
Anaesthetist Registrar, Rhyl [1969-1970]
Consultant Anaesthetist – Bangor [1985-2006]

Pat Barry joined the Anaesthetic Department in North Clwyd based in Rhyl, in August 1969 as a Registrar. She had previously worked in St Albans and only within the confines of a District General Hospital. Her first list in Llangwyfan was two to three bronchoscopies and a bronchial lavage.

She drove, what seemed a very long way from Rhyl, convinced she was lost, when suddenly it was there, "like returning to a more gracious age". The grounds were delightful with roses lining the pathways between terraced wards and the theatre block, the setting idyllic, the pace leisurely. She thought the Surgeon was Mr Hughes who had come that afternoon from Liverpool and was to return as soon as the list was finished.

She found the experience frightening initially. The Charge Nurse who assisted with the anaesthetics had done so for years and gently guided her through the established routine. This was just as well as she was unfamiliar with the serviceable but dated equipment and tubes. The tubes, including a double lumen one, went into the right orifice, patients recovered and she was rewarded with tea which was served on doilies and with china.

She was afraid to leave quickly as she was concerned about leaving recently recovered patients in a hospital **without** anaesthetic cover. What she had not appreciated was the immense experience of the Llangwyfan staff, especially Dr Biagi, who had a breadth of knowledge and experience especially looking after patients with serious chest conditions.

Working at Llangwyfan Hospital
by Dr A A Khalil MB.BCh(Cairo) DA
Anaesthetist – Associate Specialist

Over thirty years ago, approximately in the summer of 1977, I was asked to go to Llangwyfan Hospital to provide Anaesthetic care for patients who were undergoing surgical operations performed by a well known Surgeon, Mr Howell Hughes.

I arrived there in the early afternoon. It was a sunny day and I was taken aback by the impressive views of the grounds surrounding the Hospital and how well the lawn and gardens were kept.

More impressive, was the welcome I received from the staff and from Mr Hughes himself. The warm welcome I received removed all the trepidations I was experiencing and made me feel that I was amongst friends.

The session progressed safely and everything went very well. The staff worked hard and they were dedicated and kind. After finishing work we had a cup of tea and biscuits. It was a relaxed, enjoyable and rewarding experience.

At the end they were grateful and we wished each other well and I headed home to St Asaph, in a happy frame of mind. It was a heart-warming experience.

Dr Thomas Goronwy Owen MB, BCh, DA [1909-1996]
Anaesthetist – Rhyl [1960-1976]

Dr Owen visited Llangwyfan weekly when the surgical team was transferred there from Rhyl and he has been mentioned elsewhere in this book. A Welsh speaking Cardiganshire man he remained true to his roots throughout his life, promoting the Welsh language, culture and countryside. Born on the 1st October 1909 he went to Cardiff and qualified from the Welsh National School of Medicine in 1935, gaining the DA in 1954.

His medical studies were interrupted by family illness which necessitated his taking responsibility for the family grocery business, which taught him to be meticulous with finance and to make daily notes of his practice. His first appointment was with infectious diseases, then he joined the RAMC and travelled extensively. On discharge from the Army he realised after undertaking locums that he didn't want a career in General Practice and decided to try anaesthesia.

After various appointments in England including the Liverpool Anaesthetic Course he came to Rhyl in 1960 and stayed until his retirement in 1976, having given over 20,000 anaesthetics. He kept diaries where he noted where he worked each day and what anaesthetics he had given. He gave the last anaesthetic for Ivor Lewis, a patient who had a perforated duodenal ulcer at 6:30 am one morning. When they finished they had a cup of tea and bacon and egg, and at the end Mr Lewis had said "now I have finished". Dr Owen did not realise the significance of this until later. Mr Lewis had succeeded in working until he was 75 when his contract had been terminated by the Welsh Hospital Board.

He had the honour of anaesthetising Lewis Valentine for Mr O Daniel and had told me that he could not have done a bad job as Lewis Valentine lived for many years after that.

He and his wife of almost 50 years, Tilda, had one daughter,

Rhian FRCP, who became a Consultant in Palliative Care followed by an appointment as Consultant in Care of the Elderly.

I always spoke Welsh to him. He was very much a family man of integrity and a much loved and respected member of the Anaesthetic Department and community in Prestatyn where he lived. We always regarded him as "a safe pair of hands".

Dr Tim Webb FRCA

Consultant Anaesthetist – Ysbyty Glan Clwyd [1977-2008]

Dr Webb wrote:

"When I came up to North Wales in 1977 I found myself with "Just a session with Mr Howell Hughes" (later to expand to sessions with Mr Richard Doyle as well) in Llangwyfan Hospital. I had heard of Llangwyfan as the place that surgery had moved to after an outbreak of infection in patients in the Royal Alexander Hospital.

The Hospital at the time was perhaps quieter than in its hey day but still had a steady stream of patients from as far afield as Aberystwyth and Anglesey, and still had a comprehensive lung function testing unit. There were students on elective placement from Germany. It was distinctly smaller than the Swansea Hospitals that I had been working in but had that feel that I had when I had driven "over the mountain" to anaesthetise for a Surgeon from Llanelli in Amman Valley Hospital; very much a disappearing world in terms of hospital practice nowadays.

Patients had Bronchoscopies and Lung operations as well as general abdominal and urological surgery by Mr Doyle. All these operations are now concentrated in major hospitals with lung operations confined to specialist centres.

Staffing was thinner than is now the case; in hospitals elsewhere we had trained Operating Department Assistants (ODAs) who organised things for the Anaesthetist. In Llangwyfan they said "Tommy will help you". Tommy was Tommy Tynon, one of the Porters. He always had a big grin and was very willing, but not trained. I wondered why sometimes he seemed not to understand my requests, until I did a quick simple hearing test – a pair of hearing aids sorted that out. Tommy came down to Ysbyty Glan Clwyd as a Porter after Llangwyfan closed. Another transplant to Glan Clwyd was Doris Roberts, Dr Biagi's Administrator. She always seemed quiet but when she finally retired they needed several people to cope with the workload that she had taken on.

Eventually, as the Hospital was being "wound down" in preparation for Glan Clwyd to take over, the Theatre Nursing Staff was seconded from Abergele. I noticed that we usually had the Senior Sister and Gwyn Evans the Manager – I wondered if it was because the junior nurses felt isolated up on the hillside unless of course it was a nice afternoon out in the country.

The Theatre was of its era with large glass windows looking out up the hillside to let as much light in as possible. Often the cats that lived around the Hospital would play in the sun. I once wondered about taking one of a pair of beautiful tortoiseshell kittens home to my girls, but Dr Biagi said they would never become tame – he had tried in the past.

The Anaesthetic equipment differed to the rest of the Hospitals in the area. Llangwyfan had a big Blease Pulmoflator Ventilator, (breathing machine). This works by balancing the pressure in two sides of a box with a diaphragm in between which changes from breathing in to breathing out. The timing was adjusted by controlled air leaks between the two sides. As all the controls affected each other and adjusting it was quite an art, it was fortunate that I had used one before. This was in the pre-electronic era. Looking around I found another Blease machine modified for intensive care with sterilisable bellows. A plaque announced that this machine had been donated to Llangwyfan Hospital by Liverpool Football Club.

As part of my habit to relax the patients I tend to chat about anything but their operation. This had an interesting effect one day. The patient was a farmer and I being interested in my garden said that I was looking for some muck for the vegetable patch. After the list was finished I wandered around the ward to make sure that they were all well before I set off home – but there was no sign of the farmer – "He ran off home as soon as he was awake. He said he was going to keep an eye on his muck heap in case you came to steal any", they told me.

Howell Hughes would happily operate on most parts of the body – he only ever looked worried when we were dilating oesophageal strictures – in case we perforated the oesophagus. Mr Doyle used to arrive in a little MG Midget complete with a frock coat and bowler hat. Until the appointment of Miss Christine Evans he was the only Specialist Urological Surgeon working in the area. the Open Retropubic Prostatectomies that he had pioneered in Liverpool are notorious for bleeding but I do not recollect ever having to transfuse any of his patients. Aftercare was provided by Dr Biagi and his team.

Another Tale:
After the War, Nurses were imported from Germany to Llangwyfan to help with the shortages. One of these fell for a German farm worker in the village who had arrived as a Prisoner of War. In due course they wed and had a daughter, Sue. After the passage of time they died and Sue was asked "What do you want to do with the ashes?", "Oh Llangwyfan Church Yard". There seemed to be a lot of ashes to scatter – "Oh I kept mum and dad's ashes and have put the two together to scatter as it was in the churchyard that they did all their courting".

And Another:
Down by the Marsh Road Council Estate was a Dental Clinic where I provided anaesthesia for extractions and, later more

extensive work. I did not believe that patients should move straight from being anaesthetised to sitting, vomiting into a bowl, and wanted a place where they could lie down until ready to get up. After much nagging, a trolley finally turned up. It had three wheels and tipped one end up by 15 degrees or so. I enquired where it had come from as I had seen nothing quite like it in Theatres before. Finally, the answer came – it was the Mortuary trolley from Llangwyfan! Eventually equipped with a mattress it served us well for several years, I don't know what the patients would have thought if they had known.

They say that the story of people going grey overnight is a myth but a similar event occurred to a colleague some years ago.

The colleague was a Surgeon who came from the far away city to operate at Llangwyfan. He was past retiring age but his contract predated the NHS and was one of those contracts that there was no way of terminating. He used to arrive at the Hospital in an MG Midget sports car, wearing a bowler hat and frock coat. In the past he had been to Spain fighting bulls so the NHS administration was easily dodged. It seemed that there was no way to stop him operating but there was a cunning plan; we would shut the Hospital because we had a brand spanking new and, as we later discovered fire code failing, asbestos stuffed, Hospital. There was no need for Llangwyfan. However, closing Hospitals is easier said than done, so Llangwyfan carried on and its visiting Surgeons carried on coming until its Medical Superintendent reached the time to retire.

"This is the last list here" I said "I'll miss you."

"No, no" he said, "I have patients ready for next week."

"I am afraid Dr Biagi is retiring on Friday so they will be shutting the Hospital."

"Shutting the Hospital?"

"Yes – they are not replacing Dr Biagi."

Before my eyes his face fell, he seemed to look old and grey; then I noticed the edges of the frock coat were suddenly tatty and frayed, the material worn, the ribbon binding around the bowler's brim worn and the pile now shiny in patches. A look at the little sports car revealed rust everywhere.

I know that they didn't just become frayed – there was no sudden swarm of moths – It was just that before his enthusiasm shone out so you didn't notice the worn bits.

Sometimes I have come across patients who had previously been the main support of a sick spouse. When the spouse dies within a few weeks they too were admitted and died, riddled with cancer. Had their enthusiasm that had been expended to sustain their loved one kept the body apparently whole?

After a little while I asked what would he be doing next week – "Oh, I have a list at the Convent on Monday". The face lifted and the smile returned and he resumed his 10 years younger look. The hat and coat were not so fortunate."

Dr Tim Webb was born and educated in South West Birmingham before studying Medicine in Cardiff. His anaesthetic career started in Swansea and apart from a few months spent in Hong Kong his anaesthetic training was in Cardiff and Swansea. He was recruited to North Wales by Buddug Owen during a trip down Bersham coal mine organised by the Society of Anaesthetists of Wales as part of its summer meeting.

CHAPTER 7

GENERAL PRACTITIONERS

Introduction

The inaugural meeting of Clwyd and Deeside HMC was held in
the Council Offices in Prestatyn on the 18th May 1948. This was
before the NHS was formally started on the 5th July 1948. At
this meeting Huw T Edwards was in the Chair and the
Committee Members included the following medical men:
R D Aiyar – an ENT Surgeon of Chester, Dr Ivor H Davies of
Cerrigydrudion, Dr F S Hawkins (Llangwyfan), and Dr H H
Holmes a General Practitioner in St Asaph and also for a time an
Anaesthetist in Llangwyfan and C Robinson, a Dental
Practitioner of Colwyn Bay. Dr Holmes later relinquished his
General Practice to take a Senior Hospital Medical Officer post
in Obstetrics and Gynaecology in St Asaph General Hospital,
which later became HM Stanley Hospital. The HMC was given a
civic welcome by the Chairman of Prestatyn UDC, Councillor
Norman Stewart. The Assistant Senior Administrative Medical
Officer of the Welsh Regional Hospital Board, Dr Stenner Evans,
was also present. On the 22nd June 1948 William Roberts was
appointed Secretary and Supplies Officer at a salary of £1,070
rising by annual increments of £35 to a maximum of £1,420 per
year.

The Finance Committee of Llangwyfan and Denbigh
Infirmary included R D Aiyar, Dr Ivor Davies, Col Gronwy R
Griffiths, Dr F S Hawkins, Ald Mrs C Lloyd JP, and Ald T J
Roberts JP.

A House Committee for Llangwyfan was proposed on the 30th July 1948 and again included a medical man, Dr T O Jones of Ruthin, who was a General Practitioner. The House Committee was set up to examine the requisition of supplies, institute a rota of visitors and encourage the continuation of existing voluntary services to the library, canteens, linen guilds, entertainment of patients and similar forms of help.

The Chairman of the Committee became Councillor Arthur Jones. On the 10th December 1948 they agreed that central heating should be supplied to Cwyfan and Tan Rhiw. On the 11th March 1949 the Committee noted with regret that Sir Edmund Spriggs of Ruthin Castle, a Physician and supporter of Llangwyfan, had died.

All these medical practitioners have died, but I am grateful to other General Practitioners who have all now retired, for giving me what recollections they have of Llangwyfan and Tuberculosis.

Dr Edward Davies, Cerrig y Drudion OBE MB, ChB [1950-1986]

Dr Davies entered General Practice in Cerrig in 1950 and became a Partner with Dr Ifor Davies who was the third generation of his family in the Practice. His grandfather, Dr John Davies, had started the Practice, then his father Dr Huw Hughes Davies had taken over, followed by Dr Ifor – whose children did not follow him into medicine. However, Anne, his daughter, became a Social Worker and later Chairman of Clwyd Health Authority [1990-1996]. One son Glyn died in his fifties and another, Hugh, has now retired having been a Director of Technical Services in Cymdeithas Tai Clwyd Housing Association. Dr Ifor Davies was interviewed and made a tape of his life but does not mention Llangwyfan. He does, however, mention the Clement Davies Report on the importance of cleanliness of houses which he found was important when he arrived to become a rural General Practitioner in Cerrig in 1926. Mrs Ifor Davies was a Founder Member of the League of Friends of Llangwyfan.

Dr Eddie spoke warmly of Dr Ifor Davies, describing him as a wise man with whom he never had a cross word in 22 years of working together. Dr Ifor was involved with many committees including the Clwyd and Deeside HMC, BMA and Secretary of the LMC. In the first few years Dr Eddie was in practice the old patients with Tuberculosis were looked after at home and very few patients were sent to Llangwyfan. There was a Chest Clinic in Wrexham run by Dr Clifford Jones and 95% of his patients were referred to Wrexham, not Bangor, with all his TB patients going to this Chest Clinic which was run by Denbighshire County Council. He was impressed by Dr Clifford Jones, although he never met him, and thought him a very good clinician.

He was surprised how little TB there was around when he arrived at Cerrig, although in his book "Moddion o Fag y Meddyg" he quotes statistics between 1785 and 1791 of the 96 people who died, 31 having had Tuberculosis. By the 1950's when Streptomycin was used some patients had short term admission to Llangwyfan, whereas now they are treated as out-patients so the need for sanatoria declined.

In the early days Eddie's wife, Sibyl, would accompany Mrs Ifor Davies to the summer fetes in Llangwyfan which were supported by people from a very wide area. She was impressed as a nurse by the standard of care provided by the Hospital when their son was operated on by Mr Ivor Lewis for removal of a Branchial Cyst in the late 1960's and was an in-patient for four to five days.

Although Tuberculosis was declining, the incidence of Farmers Lung was rising and he remembers a smallholding housewife developing it after working with mouldy hay. Many housewives did a considerable amount to assist their husbands with farming tasks or when widowed.

When he arrived at Cerrig, cancer of the stomach was prevalent and he had 17 patients with it, five of whom presented with secondary deposits in the brain.

Dr Davies was Editor of 'Cennad', a Welsh Medical Journal for a number of years and is a past President of 'Y Gymdeithas Feddygol', a Welsh Medical Society as well as 'The History of Medicine Society of Wales". For his work to his community he was honoured with an OBE. He is also a Member of the White Order of Bards of the National Eisteddfod of Wales. He published a book on the North Wales Quarry Hospitals in 2003 as well as 'Moddion o Fag y Meddyg (Medicine from the Doctors Bag)' in 2005 and had previously published a book in Welsh on First Aid. He had been involved with St John's Ambulance for over 50 years and was made a Knight of that Order. His knowledge of Welsh medical history is encyclopaedic, although I was surprised when he told me that until he had read my book he had not known that there had been a school in Llangwyfan.

He draws out in 'Moddion o Fag y Meddyg' the poverty of the area where he was working – doctors were paid 'in kind' often, not in money. Uwchaled was a community of scattered villages and in the 19th Century the cottages were one room, where a family of husband and wife lived with four to five children. There was a stone hearth with open fire burning peat and the rest of the room had an earth floor where the family lived and slept. Diet was poor, mostly carbohydrate with vegetables and fruit scarce. It was an ideal breeding ground for Tuberculosis and the incidence was high with many dying young. Chronic Tuberculosis was nursed at home, Dr Eddie had told me when he arrived in Cerrig.

Dr Cyril William Lewis Jones
MB, BS (Lond), MRCS, LRCP
General Practitioner in Ruthin [1951-1988]

Having seen an advertisement for a General Practitioner in Ruthin, at a time when getting a post in General Practice was difficult, Dr Bill Lewis Jones applied and was interviewed in London by Dr Henry Jones, whose father Dr Thomas Owen Jones had been a General Practitioner in Ruthin for 60 years and had started the Practice. He was successful and enjoyed the 37 years he spent in this delightful part of the world where the medical fraternity got on well with each other.

Dr Lewis Jones told me that he had had a lot to do with Llangwyfan. When Dr Roger Altouynian, a Chest Physician of Manchester who was of Turkish descent visited Llangwyfan, Dr Biagi would organise a clinical meeting there which he and his partner Dr Magor Winstanley, along with Mr Ivor Lewis, Dr Gallagher and Dr Cameron, would attend to discuss patients and their treatment. Dr Lewis Jones attended four or five of these, more or less yearly, lasting 1–1½ hours. Dr Biagi would also make domiciliary visits to see patients in their own homes and provided a very good service.

Dr T O Jones was held in very high regard by patients who came to Ruthin Castle Clinic. One patient, a regular attendee with ulcerative colitis, when he rang to book a bed in the clinic asked that Dr T O Jones be asked to come and see him to give him his treatment of Parathyroid and Calcium which was always successful.

Ruthin Castle Clinic was a well known private clinic and advertisements about it regularly appeared in the British Medical Journal so that Dr Lewis Jones had heard of it. It was a well run clinic which had very good X-ray and Biochemical Departments. The Radiologist, Dr Marxer, was excellent and had been involved in his speciality from the beginning. The clinic had been transferred from Banff in Scotland when the lease on premises there expired and was under the Medical Director, Sir Edward Spriggs, who was also an Honorary Member of staff of Llangwyfan. It closed in the late 1950's or early 1960's and was sold for around £29k.

Dr Lewis Jones' father had been a patient in Llangwyfan and one night Dr Jones had received a phone call at 11:00 pm to say that he wasn't at all well. When he got to the hospital his father had an oxygen mask on his face, which he took off to tell his son "damn it Bill, they've taken away my matches". Probably the last words he spoke, as at 6:00 am the following morning he died. The importance of keeping flames away from oxygen is mentioned in another chapter.

Dr Bill had been born in Burryport where his father was a Teacher and after twelve months had moved to Gowerton. Later his father was Headmaster at Pontardulais. Bill went to the Elementary School and then to Tregwyr County School which was referred to by Dr Phil Williams, in a Science Week in Wrexham as one of the best schools in Wales, which made him feel very proud. This was the school that Karl Jenkins, the Composer, and Dr Greenway of Ysbyty Glan Clwyd, had also attended.

He did his 1st MB at Swansea Technical College which he said was excellent, combining training for veterinary medicine, medicine and pharmacy. He did his medical training at the London Hospital which during the war was transferred to Cambridge for two years, and qualified in 1946. After house jobs in London he joined the Army for National Service, being deployed in East Africa.

He had done a student house job in the North Middlesex, with Ivor Lewis, and gave general anaesthetics for Mr Lewis to undertake surgery – a great privilege. He thought Ivor Lewis ruled the Hospital with a rod of iron but was very fair.

When he arrived in British Swaziland (East Africa), he found conditions very primitive and did all the surgery as he had been graded a surgeon. When he returned home he became a Surgical Registrar in Gloucester and took Part I FRCS. He had tried to get a variety of posts to equip him for life as a General Practitioner and settling in Ruthin he found a large catchment area. He had not found a conflict in deciding which patients should go to Llangwyfan and which to Ruthin Hospital. There was a move at one time to close small hospitals, but Ruthin survived and the Chief Nursing Officer for Wales had supported them. Dr Eddie Davies would undertake the antenatal care of patients in Cerrigydrudion and for delivery the mother would be admitted to Ruthin Hospital and looked after by Dr Bill and his colleagues. Dr Magor Winstanley arrived in Ruthin after Dr Bill, but he died on his retirement some 20 years ago.

When Dr Bill arrived in Ruthin he was taken by Dr T O Jones to Llangwyfan to meet Dr Hawkins, who left to take up another post shortly afterwards. His place was taken by Dr Biagi who provided them with a very good service. Gertie Hughes, whose photograph appears in Llangwyfan as a Dispenser, worked for a time in their practice in Ruthin. She was born in Anglesey and on leaving Ruthin moved to work in Llangwyfan. She was also a very good Red Cross worker.

Patients were sent to see Dr Clifford Jones in the Chest Clinic for Denbighshire County Council in Wrexham and seen by him or his Deputy, Dr Lovegreen.

Dr Lewis Jones' wife, **Haf**, a Law Graduate, was a supporter of Llangwyfan attending the Hospital's charity events. She was a Member of the House Committee, which she thought very worthwhile and it had a very good Chairman – Lewis Lloyd who was the Anglesey Representative of the North Wales Hospital, Denbigh and through this connection was seconded to Llangwyfan. Dr David Jones attended from Clwyd Health Authority; Mrs W A Evans who was Dr Morton Evans of

Denbigh's mother, Mrs Henry Hughes and Dr Bruce Jackson were all very supportive.

She became Vice-Chairman of the Action Group called to keep Llangwyfan open. For the first few meetings many organisations were represented but afterwards numbers dropped. She said that Edgar Hughes, Treasurer of Denbighshire County Council, was a good member and I told her that his sister Anita Hughes had kept an Autograph Book when a patient in Llangwyfan in 1923, and is mentioned in Vol I of this book. She told me that he was an "annwyl" man (a dear man), sound and good.

Councillor John Hughes of Llangernyw was also very good and sound. Ieuan Wyn Jones AM who won the Welsh Politician of the Year Award in 2007 in ITV's Wales Annual Political Awards was supportive. Ieuan Wyn Jones at this time was Plaid Cymru Leader and Deputy First Minister in the Assembly.

She remembers attending an early AGM of the League of Friends when the Guest Speaker was Ann Clwyd who told the audience she wanted to be a Politician – the first time she had heard anyone say this. There was a Library Sub-Committee with various organisations taking it in turn to take the books around the wards each week.

She also heard Llangwyfan described as "Y Llan uchel llawn iechyd" by Trevor Davies of Llanynys ("The high Llan full of Health").

Dr John Bernard Lynch
OBE, MB Ch.B (Manch) MRCS, LRCP, MRCGP
General Practitioner, Denbigh [1960-1991]

Dr Lynch qualified in Manchester in 1956 and after house jobs did 2 years in the RAMC 1957-1959. From 1959-1960 he became a Junior Hospital Medical Officer in Colwyn Bay Hospital, joining The Beech House Surgery, Denbigh in July 1960 as a

General Medical Practitioner where he remained throughout his professional life, retiring on ill-health in 1991. He became a Police Surgeon for Denbigh and the Medical Officer looking after staff at HM Stanley Hospital, St Asaph.

He referred about one patient a month to Llangwyfan sometimes following a Domiciliary Consultation by Dr Biagi or Dr Gallagher. Mostly these were patients with chest problems, influenza, cardiac problems or kidney malfunction. Dr Biagi attended at Denbigh Infirmary weekly to see referred patients. There was a very good professional relationship between the General Practitioners and easy access to Dr Biagi and Dr Gallagher. If the patient remained at home both of these doctors would be available to offer advice and this remained until both had retired.

There was a weekly meeting for Denbigh and Ruthin GP's at Llangwyfan, where discussion was open and questions encouraged and answered. Whilst Ruthin GP's were in the forefront of the fight to keep Llangwyfan open the Denbigh GP's, though supportive, were fighting to retain The Denbigh Infirmary.

In 1968, because of his interest in anaesthesia, he joined the Anaesthetic Department based at the Royal Alexandra Hospital, Rhyl as a Clinical Assistant. After training he gave anaesthetics at the North Wales Hospital, Denbigh for ECT; The Rhyl Hospitals, HM Stanley Hospital and Abergele Hospital. He also gave anaesthetics for local dental surgeons and at the Denbigh Infirmary. He became a Member of the Hospital Medical Staff Committee in Rhyl and the Denbigh Infirmary Medical Committee. All these activities gave him a wide knowledge of medical matters across the area and in 1968 he started his medico-political career in the Local Medical Committee. He was Honorary Secretary of the West Denbigh Division of the BMA for about 6 years and later Chairman of Clwyd North BMA Division in 1983.

In 1971 he became a Member of the Welsh General Medical

Services Committee, and in 1982 a Member of The General Medical Services Committee (GMSC) for England, Northern Ireland and Scotland. He was a Member of the Welsh Medical Committee and Chairman of its GP Advisory Sub-Committee.

From 1985 – 1991 he was a GMSC negotiator and became Vice-Chairman of the GMSC in 1988. In 1991 he was appointed to the UK Standing Medical Advisory Committee by the Department of Health, Medicines Control Agency.

In 1990 he was Chairman of the Welsh Council of the BMA and was widely tipped to become Chairman of the GMSC, but Dr Ian Bogle was the successful candidate. It was felt in retrospect that he had the more aggressive approach as Dr Lynch had been described in the medical press as having "a non-aggressive negotiating approach" and "that he avoided confrontational bargaining". He was a superb General Practitioner and his sudden catastrophic illness deprived all his patients of his talents and the BMA in particular of a skilled, fair negotiator and Chairman. His services to medicine in Wales were honoured with an OBE in 1992. His membership of the Welsh Computer Strategy Committee and his knowledge of IT has been a tremendous help to him to communicate following his illness and this has been an inspiration to his many friends.

Dr Gwyn Thomas, Denbigh MB, BCh, FRCGP

Gwyn Thomas' mother, Nest Owen Thomas [1900-1988] and her sister Eled, both qualified as Dental Surgeons in Liverpool in the 1920's. They were 2 of 5 children of Dr Owen Jones and his wife, Dr Owen Jones being a General Practitioner in Holywell who lived in some style – with maids, a cook and seamstress. There were two other girls, twins, one of whom studied music and got her LRAM and the other domestic science. Also one boy who died in his 50's when Gwyn was a student.

A cousin of Gwyn's, Hugh Owen Thomas, an Orthopaedic Surgeon in Liverpool, is looking into their family tree and there may be a connection between Gwyn's father and mother. All of Dr Owen Jones' children were well educated and went to college.

Gwyn's father, John Griffith Thomas [1890-1968], was born in Cyffylliog; the son of an Innkeeper who also had shops; and was one of 11 children. He was a well known character and General Practitioner in Denbigh, who never took a holiday and was a distant father whilst his wife I was told was a fantastic mother.

He opened a Branch Surgery in Llansannan in the front room of Aled House and patients waited in a passageway outside the room which had a gas stove for heating. He always turned up late and indeed always took his meals late, always being one meal behind the rest of the family throughout the day. He was interested in Welsh poetry and won a prize in the Llanrwst Eisteddfod for the best englyn. A great talker he became known as "the late Dr Thomas".

He did not talk about Llangwyfan with Gwyn and he was never seen talking to Dr Biagi. The question was posed "had they fallen out?", but without an answer. He was never invited to Llangwyfan parties, but Gwyn and his brother Deri went and performed a duo "the one armed fiddler", which proved so popular they were invited back to perform it every year.

Dr Gwyn Thomas has written an entertaining autobiography and in it mentioned that he had a patient with poliomyelitis who was treated in an Iron Lung, and I wondered if this was in Llangwyfan, but found she had been sent to Wrexham. Dr Thomas said he had never seen an Iron Lung and I have had conflicting reports – one of a room full of Iron Lungs in Llangwyfan, and another of never seeing one there. Neither did he have patients who had been in North Wales Hospital for mental diseases, Denbigh and then sent to Llangwyfan. He mentions Mr Sutcliffe Kerr of Liverpool doing Leucotomies under local analgesia in Denbigh and I was able to tell him that at one time

I had given the patients general anaesthesia to have this operation carried out by Mr Sutcliffe Kerr.

Dr Thomas told me that Professor Howard Harvard Davies had said that South Wales patients were sent to Llangwyfan and North Wales patients were sent to Talgarth so that they wouldn't have visitors often and therefore there was less chance of Tuberculosis spreading in the families. I haven't seen this written as policy or suggestion in any original material I've studied.

Professor J G Jones wondered why his mother Catherine and friend went to Llangwyfan to train and not Talgarth. Certainly, Catherine never went home during her two years in Llangwyfan and therefore her mother, who didn't want her to nurse TB patients, might have felt there was less chance of her infecting the rest of the family if she went further away.

CHAIRMEN OF CLWYD & DEESIDE HMC

Huw T Edwards JP, LL.D [1892-1970]
Chairman Clwyd and Deeside Hospital Management
Committee [1948-1967]

There is only one referral in Gwyn Jenkins' biography of Huw T
Edwards to the fact that he was Chairman of Clwyd and Deeside
Hospital Management Committee and a Member of the Welsh
Regional Hospital Board.

I remember him well as a charming, charismatic, short man
with a rugged face and big sensual mouth. An ardent Welshman,
he was always very friendly and always spoke to me in Welsh. He
had achieved a great deal in his life and was regarded, as the
biography indicates, the uncrowned Prime Minister of Wales.
Clwyd and Deeside were lucky to have him as their first
Chairman under the National Health Service.

He was born on the 19th November 1892, his ancestors coming
from the Tal y Fan area 4 miles from Conwy. They were mountain
people and farm servants and his father was a breaker of stones
in Penmaenmawr quarry. His mother died when he was eight
and he did not like his new step-mother; becoming a rebel and
described in the school log book of 1906 as a "very badly
conducted boy". He left school shortly afterwards to work in
Graiglwyd Quarry, Penmaenmawr. He then became a Farm
Labourer and moved to South Wales to become a Miner earning

12 shillings a week. He joined the Army Special Reserve for 6 years and when the Senghennydd pit fire occurred in 1913 killing 439 people, he went down the pit to look for survivors. He was called up to join the Army on the 4th August 1914 and in March 1918 was badly injured on the Somme. He became a socialist and pacifist but was never a religious man.

He married in 1920 and founded the Penmaenmawr Labour Party in 1924, being appointed Secretary and learnt the craft of public speaking. He described it as the "University of Penmaenmawr". He stood as a Labour Councillor in 1927 and was Chair of the Council by 1932. At this time he had developed his literary streak and had started composing plays and poetry. He gave talks, mainly in Welsh, on radio and television. In 1932 he was appointed Secretary of the Transport and General Workers Union for North Wales and moved to live in Shotton which, at that time, was the economic centre of North Wales. He became an Alderman of Flintshire County Council in 1939 with a high reputation for being fair and giving sound judgement.

He was honoured with an MBE in 1943 but sent it back in 1945 and turned down subsequent honours, but accepted a Doctorate by the University of Wales in 1957. He became a Member of the Council for Wales and from 1950-1958 was its Chairman. He was in favour of Devolution for Wales.

At a meeting of Clwyd and Deeside Hospital Management Committee held on the 5th May 1949 Alderman G O Williams MBE, JP, congratulated the Chairman Huw T Edwards on his honour conferred by the Prime Minister of being appointed the first Chairman of the recently constituted Advisory Council for Wales.

Huw T, as he was affectionately known to Hospital Staff, was approachable and a good communicator. The Colwyn Bay House Committee Minutes of the 2nd December 1948, the year he took up his appointment, note that at the end of the meeting he had given an address explaining to the Members of the Committee the structure of the hospital service under the NHS Act 1946 and detailed the functions of the House Committee.

He as Chairman, along with the Vice-Chairman, was an ex-officio member of all committees and sub-committees and obviously took these duties seriously, attending when he was able to do so despite his busy schedule.

He was an author, his first book "Tros y Tresi" is the story of his life from his roots to the leadership of Trade Unions and the Leadership of the Nation as Chairman of the Council for Wales. His second book "It Was My Privilege" is the history of the growth of the Transport and General Workers Union in North Wales. At the end of the book he makes no apology for his Welshness and states he is proud of his Welsh contribution in the field of human endeavour and care of the "Bottom Dog".

William Armon Ellis OBE, LLB (1913-1994)
Chairman of Clwyd & Deeside Hospital Management
Committee [1967-1974]

Armon Ellis was born in Lixwm, Flintshire on the 29th February 1913, celebrating his birthday on St David's Day. He attended the village school followed by the county school in Holywell. When he left school he worked for a couple of years for an uncle as a builder/plasterer. He then went to the University College of Wales, Aberystwyth as a mature student where, in the 1930's, he got a 1st Class Honours in Law. During this time he worked hard, did not join societies and was in the same year as William Mars Jones, the eminent High Court Judge, who was knighted. During this time he was not obvious in the social life of the college.

Afterwards, he was articled for 3 years to a good Solicitors Firm in Mold – Llewelyn Jones, at the end of which he took his final examination in 1939. He was in the Army during the war and on demobilisation opened an office in Rhyl on the corner of Brighton Road and Paradise Street. After the war he was not so shy and started to take an interest in Court work as well as maintaining his link with Llewelyn Jones. After the elder Partner in the firm died, his work in Mold increased but he kept the Rhyl Office open.

In the 1950's – 1960's he became a County Councillor for Lixwm where he did well and became well known. He stood as a Liberal candidate for Flintshire on one occasion and made close friendships with other prominent men on the Council.

He carried a heavy work commitment and pushed himself, being a very able man. Even so, because of this, there was surprise that he was able to take on the Chair of Clwyd and Deeside Hospital Management Committee 1967-1974 with his other demanding work. He was an approachable man and made himself available to meet as many staff and patients as possible who wanted to talk to him. He was a heavy smoker and developed heart problems, and after his second wife's death he was admitted to a Nursing Home on more than one occasion. He died on the 6th November 1994.

When the Action Group was formed to keep Llangwyfan open he was elected the Chairman. With his political links and command of the Welsh language, he again proved a popular choice, well liked and trusted by everyone.

Lewis Hunt – Group Secretary

Lewis Hunt arrived in Rhyl as Group Secretary of the hospitals in the area of North Clwyd in the middle of the 1960's and retired in 1982. He saw the transition of Clwyd and Deeside Hospital Management Committee under the Chairmanship of Huw T Edwards and W Armon Ellis until 1974; followed by Clwyd Health Authority Chairman Lord Kenyan 1974-1978, Dr Emyr

Wyn Jones 1978-1980, and the start of Michael Griffith's Chairmanship 1980-1990.

He remembers the pleasure of going to Llangwyfan where everything appeared gentle and friendly; and where the surrounding countryside was beautiful. He and Ruth, his wife, often walked in the hills behind the Hospital and enjoyed the vista and peace of this area of outstanding natural beauty.

He was always conscious of the fact that there was always so much to do and never enough money to carry out everything. He does not remember problems between the Area and District Management Teams and was on friendly terms with Don Cope, the Area Chief Executive. He knew him from their days in Yorkshire and Don had attended Lewis and Ruth's wedding. He said that Don was "dyed in the wool Yorkshire", a man who was bright and had struggled hard, moving around in order to advance his career. He remembered Armon Ellis as a prominent, political, Welsh and charming man who got on well with everyone and was anxious to visit the hospitals. Lord Kenyon was a more private man and though he didn't get to know him well, he took him to visit the new hospital developments in Rhyl and felt he knew what the service needed and tried to get this accomplished.

Llangwyfan Fading Memories by Malcolm Pratt
Group Engineer [1970-1981]

My association with the Sanatorium goes back to the 1970's when the North Wales Mental Health Management Committee (HMC) was divided amongst the Acute HMC's, and I emerged from the exercise as Group Engineer for the Clwyd and Deeside HMC under the Chairmanship of H T Edwards, with Peter Royce as Group Secretary.

The care and maintenance of the building services at Llangwyfan were under my wing until the site was closed.

The Hospital had been under closure threat for many years, with the planning of the new District General Hospital at Glan Clwyd. Hence, the resources for running and maintaining the services were virtually non-existent. Like most Hospital planning the due process became truncated, with the result that the Hospital's services became more and more dilapidated. If it were not for the exceptional skills of the Hospital Engineer Alec Sinclair, the services would have ceased to function much sooner than they did. Alec was a Scotsman, ex-Merchant Navy Engineer, with an amazing ability to make do and mend.

The drinking water supply came from a spring at the rear of the Hospital, with the only filtration through a gravel bed into a large storage/header tank. The source must have been good as statutory testing never showed any problems. The water supply for the boilers, laundry, steam generation etc came from a much more dubious source and gave cause for major concern, particularly on one occasion when the supply became polluted from a pig farm upstream. This gave rise to a new water main being brought to the Hospital and the two water sources closed down except for the staff houses on the northern extremities of the site. This is where I lived at Islwyn, along with Bill Owen at Penllwyn. Miss Behrans lived at the bottom house, Erw Vran, along with her pack of beagles.

Another memory takes me back to the heating distribution, which was carried through ducts which ran around the site, and were covered in concrete slabs. These ducts provided a network of walkways. The pipe insulation was so poor that after snowfall the snow would melt on the duct covers giving clear walkways around between all the buildings without have to resort to manual snow clearance or gritting. On very cold days heating and hot water would hardly reach the top wards and we would have to resort to using electric fires. The state of the services became so bad that the whole was eventually replaced, albeit on a piecemeal basis as finance became available.

The ultimate failure came when one of the steam boilers was shut down for insurance inspection and the other collapsed, fortunately with no injury to staff. With all the skills that Alec had, the situation could not be retrieved, the insurance inspector condemned the installation, and regardless of expense temporary boilers had to be brought on site. The Contractor who carried out that installation was Sewards of Chester, whose staff worked around the clock to get everything up and running. Their Site Foreman was a metal bender by the name of Norman, who was an absolute genius at pipe bending and bonded with Alec to progress the works. The only trouble with Norman was his language, every other word was the "F" word, so after a lot of persuasion and the introduction of a swear box, Norman was prevailed upon to replace the "F" with "PI".

Although we managed to keep essential services running, the laundry was transferred to the North Wales Hospital, Denbigh and the CSSD to HM Stanley Hospital, never to return. In a way this was the start of the rundown of Llangwyfan. One benefit was the spare space, that became available with the transfer of the laundry, and Alec moved in to give himself a much deserved increase in office space.

All this of course did not happen in isolation. Bill Owen, Hospital Secretary, was involved in negotiating the transfer of the laundry services. However, the greatest influence was Matron Blod Morris, whose Assistants sorted out storage for the clean laundry and CSSD and the management of the process. In a way, Bill was sidelined by powerhouse Blod.

During less traumatic times, once a month, I was invited to lunch with Blod and her girls. Bill Owen was rarely invited, and was not impressed when I would have a meeting with him in the morning, and then have lunch with Blod whilst he went to the canteen. He never clicked that Blod and I were devout South Walians and with the friendliness of the Clan, I always called her by her Christian name, whereas with Bill it would be "yes Matron, no Matron".

These lunches were something to remember, even now I drool at the prospect. We always had soup, a roast that Blod would carve and serve, plenty of vegetables all in tureens, followed up with a steamed pudding and custard, all preceded by a glass of sweet sherry. The Chef was always summoned for us to praise, and prompted by Blod made sure we had not left any vegetables. Blod was a good listener and over lunch I would tell her about the problems on site, how wonderful Alec was and the frustrations there were at not being properly funded. During her rounds she would always seek out Alec and kept herself fully briefed.

Another honour was to be Blod's guest at the Staff Christmas Party. It was always a black tie job for those invited. Blod would lay on a wonderful spread, with all the local great and the good invited, along with the members of the HMC and those from various charities who helped out during the year. Blod would look resplendent in a figure-hugging taffeta ball gown, and had such tenacity dancing with all her male guests in turn.

Moving on to a more personal memory, a friend of mine and his wife Kit came over from Canada to stay with us. When Kit was a child living in Aberystwyth, she had to spend a year as a patient in Llangwyfan, and she asked me to take her on a nostalgia trip to the Sanatorium. Needless to say we bumped into Blod who was doing a round with her deputies. Straight away she said "Hello Kate", not Kit, "how are you". She recognised Kit straight away after nearly twenty years. You can imagine the conversation as we retired to Blod's office for tea and scones. We were there for nearly two hours.

CHAIRMEN OF CLWYD HEALTH AUTHORITY

Clwyd Health Authority
Lord Kenyon (1917-) LLD, DL
Chairman, Clwyd Health Authority [1974-1978]

Lord Kenyon had had considerable experience of involvement with the Health Service for around 20 years before becoming Chairman of Clwyd Health Authority. He was a Member of the Welsh Regional Hospital Board 1958-1963, Council for Professions Supplementary to Medicine 1961-1965, and Chairman of Wrexham, Powys and Mawddch Hospital Management Committee 1960-1974.

He was the 5th Baron Kenyon, educated at Eton and Magdalene College Cambridge gaining a BA in 1950 following Army service in the Royal Artillery, retiring from ill-health in 1943 with Honorary Rank of Captain. He was a Director of Lloyds Bank Plc 1962-1988 and Chairman of the North West Board.

He was interested in education and the arts, being President of the University College of North Wales, Bangor 1947-1982, National Musuem of Wales 1952-1957, Trustee of the National Portrait Gallery 1966-1988 and a Friend of the National Libraries 1962-1985 as well as being Chief Commander for Wales of the Boy Scouts Association 1948-1965. He was honoured with an LLD Wales in 1958 and became a Deputy Lieutenant of the

County of Flint in 1948. He became a County Councillor of Flint in 1946 and was Chairman from 1954-1955.

An experienced Chairman it was during his time as Chairman of Clwyd Health Authority that the decision was taken to close Llangwyfan Hospital. Following widespread consultation the Secretary of State for Wales, the Right Honourable John Morris MP, made the final decision in January 1977.

Dr Emyr Wyn Jones OBE, MD, FRCP, LLD (1907-1999)
Clwyd Health Authority Chairman [1978-1980]

Dr Emyr was a much loved and respected Welshman who had been a Consultant Physician in Liverpool Royal Infirmary and Director of Cardiac Studies and Physician in charge of the Regional Cardiac Centre in Liverpool. He was a Past Chairman of the British Cardiac Society.

He was born in Waunfawr on 23 May 1907, son of the Reverend James Jones, Uwchmynydd, Llŷn, a Calvanistic Methodist Minister and of Elen Jones, Clynnog Fawr. A Welshman to his core he took every opportunity to speak the language and the people of North Wales flocked to consult him in Liverpool. He attended Caernarvon County School before proceeding to study medicine in Liverpool, where he graduated taking many scholarships and prizes. From 1938-1972 he was on the staff of the Royal Infirmary, in 1949 becoming a Fellow of the Royal College of Physicians.

In 1939 he was invited by the War Office to serve as Consultant to the North Wales Hospitals of Bangor, Rhyl and Wrexham. In 1947 he became a High Sheriff of Caernarvon and in 1972 he was appointed OBE.

He served on Clwyd Health Authority and the Welsh Regional Hospital Board, becoming Vice-Chairman of the Board and was Chairman of Clwyd Health Authority from 1978-1980. He represented the University of Wales on the Council of the Welsh National School of Medicine, Cardiff. At the University College of North Wales, Bangor he was a Council Member and Vice-President.

He received the Honorary Degree of LLD by the University of Wales and was elected Fellow of the Royal National Eisteddfod of Wales following being Chairman of its Council and President of its Court. He had also been a Member of Council of the National Library of Wales in Aberystwyth, where he had found great pleasure reading and researching for the many papers he produced in English and Welsh over the years. He had been President of Y Gymdeithas Feddygol and of the History of Medicine Society of Wales.

The decision to close Llangwyfan had been made when he became Chairman of Clwyd Health Authority and he was there when it was running down and had many staffing problems. His wisdom, fairness and steady hand helped to smooth the process. He understood the people who worked there, would listen and be able to talk to them in their native language. When we finally moved into Glan Clwyd in May 1980 I was the Chairman of the Hospital Medical Staff Committee and I organised an informal buffet meal to celebrate the fact that the move had gone so well, and invited Dr Emyr Wyn to join us and say a few words. As always, they were to the point and gracious.

E M W Griffith CBE, DL
Chairman Clwyd Health Authority [1980-1990]

The decision to close Llangwyfan had been taken before Michael Griffith became Chairman of Clwyd Health Authority, but he was in the Chair when the Authority sold the Hospital and Farm to Briggs Trantex Development. As he explained in the Foreword of Llangwyfan Sanatorium to Hospital, once he and Don Cope, the

Chief Executive, had given their word they could not renege when a higher bid was made for it.

He had been educated in Eton College followed by the Royal Agriculture College Cirencester, then followed almost thirty five years of lowland and hill farming. During this time he was Chairman of the Vale of Clwyd Farmers for six years, Member of the Agriculture Research Council for 9 years, Non-Executive Director of the North West Bank for eight years and he took an active role in the National Trust both in Wales and Nationally.

His wide experience of agriculture and nature conservancy, health and finance resulted in his becoming Chairman of the Countryside Council for Wales 1991-2000, and Chairman of Glan Clwyd District General Hospital Trust 1992-1999, followed by Chairman of Conwy and Denbighshire NHS Trust 1999-2001. He was a wise and gifted Chairman, endeavouring to encompass all viewpoints to consensus decisions. He knew his staff and would listen and talk to them when he visited hospitals and was aware of what went on at local level. His expertise was also utilised by the Welsh National School of Medicine with which he has been involved since 1997, becoming Chairman of Council. An active Christian, supportive of the Church in Wales and actively involved in his local community as well as on an all Wales level where he is Patron of the National Library, National Museum and Welsh Botanic Garden.

His interests are wide-ranging, from countryside matters as Past President of the Royal Welsh Show, Cymdeithas Edward Llwyd, Countryside Alliance, RSPB, National Trust, CPRW and Wildlife Trusts. He is Vice-President of the Cardiff Business Club and Institute of Welsh Affairs.

A true Welshman, he is descended from Owain Glyndwr and enjoys delving into historical matters as a friend of Clwyd Archives, British Library and North Wales University of Bangor, as well as the Medical School, Cardiff, Linnaean Society and Royal Society of Arts. He is always supportive of his wife's deep interest and involvement in Riding for the Disabled. He is Vice Lord-Lieutenant of Clwyd, is a past High Sheriff of Denbighshire and was honoured with a CBE in 1986.

His tremendous energy, charm, affability and humour has always been utilised for the service of others.

Area and District Officers
Professor D T Jones
Chief Administrative Medical Officer, Clwyd Health Authority

Professor Jones' account: From my schooldays at Llanrwst grammar school during the war years, I was well aware of the crucial role that Llangwyfan Hospital played in the battle against Tuberculosis, and that it was held in very high regard by the people of North Wales. Indeed, my old maths master, the late Alun Lewis, spent well over a year there in 1944/45 being treated for Pulmonary Tuberculosis. His career as a Welsh short story writer began whilst he was a patient there.

When I returned to Wales in 1971 to work for the then Welsh Regional Hospital Board, the plans for the 1974 reorganisation of the NHS were underway, and, as the Board's Medical Representative in the north, part of my job was to become involved with the planning of the new DGH's at Bodelwyddan, Bangor and Wrexham. The Welsh Hospital Board had more or less ceased to function by the late summer of 1973, and I was offered a job in Clwyd by Lord Kenyon, the then Chairman of the Wrexham, Powys and Mawddach HMC. He was acting on the advice of his HMC Secretary, Don Cope, with whom I had established a very good working relationship.

My first job with Clwyd was to write the consultation document outlining the Health Authority's plans for the hospitals in Clwyd following the completion and commissioning of the Bodelwyddan DGH, which was expected to occur in 1978.

The Welsh Office made it clear to us all that there would have to be hospital closures to help with the revenue to run the new hospital. Rather than just produce a list of hospitals for closure, I decided, together with my friend Wyndham Evans, Planning Officer, to put forward a strategy for the redevelopment of our hospitals in accordance with principles which we felt best suited the needs of the people in this semi-rural area.

These principles included:

1. Appropriate services to be located as near as possible to where people lived.
2. Such services had to make economic sense, i.e. to be both efficient and effective.
3. High tech/specialist services to be concentrated on the DGH's.
4. Community services to be focused on what we termed Primary Health Care Teams, centred around GP Practices.

Our document more or less wrote itself once our principles and their implications had been worked through. We developed a three tier structure, with the DGH at its centre, ringed by a number of what we termed Community Hospitals [this was based on Oxford region's pioneering work with these hospitals]. These were, in turn, supported by a number of Primary Health Care Centres.

In the Spring of 1973 or 1974 the late Dr Emyr Wyn Jones, acting in his capacity of Deputy Chairman of the Welsh Hospital Board, officiated at the 'cutting of the sod' ceremony at Bodelwyddan for the new DGH. The pressure was then really on for us to publish our proposals for the existing hospitals once the DGH opened its doors for business! Our document saw no future for Llangwyfan on a number of grounds, such as: TB had been conquered, not suited for the elderly because of its relatively isolated locations, not suited to be a community hospital because it was not central to its nearest communities of Denbigh and Ruthin.

I believe I did meet the action group, probably on more than one occasion, mainly to assure them that the new Health Authority was not in the business of making anyone redundant, and that special arrangements would be put in place to minimise any problems which individual members of staff might experience as a result of having to travel to another hospital within Clwyd. The people of Denbigh and Ruthin were also promised that considerable investment would be made in their own hospitals to enable these to function as community hospitals. My recollection is that our plans were widely welcomed, subject only to the quite natural suspicion that whilst the closures would take place, the additional facilities we had promised would not!!

Lord Kenyon was my Chairman from 1974 to 1978 and was followed by Dr Emyr Wyn until Michael Griffith took over in 1980. I was very fond of Lord Kenyon, and he was always supportive of whatever I tried to do, provided he was satisfied that it made sense. In 1981, Lord Kenyon, Don Cope and I were called before a House of Commons Select Committee to explain how an elderly lady with a fractured hip had been transferred late at night from the Prince Edward casualty unit at Rhyl to Llangwyfan where she had died shortly after. I think the young casualty doctor who ordered the transfer probably had had no idea where Llangwyfan was. The result was that the three of us were given a roasting by the Select Committee! Lord Kenyon was an aristocrat of the old school who had a strong sense of public duty to Clwyd. I believe his mother had been a most formidable Chairman of Flintshire County Council in her day.

Armon Ellis I knew from my attendances at meetings of the Clwyd and Deeside HMC. I also came to know him as a 'good liberal'. Quite an avuncular, friendly sort of chap, but I rarely came across him after 1974.

Stan Wyn Jones, OBE
Chief Administrative Nursing Officer for Clwyd Health Authority

Mr Stan Wyn Jones visited Llangwyfan approximately once a month with a Personnel Officer to sort out Industrial Relations during the last few years. He understood the feeling the staff had of working to keep Llangwyfan open, and their questioning of why the District General Hospital couldn't be built there. At the same time he thought that many had no understanding of the need to move on and keep abreast of the developments in medicine and the technological age.

In 1969-1970 Stan had worked in the Welsh Regional Hospital Board in Cardiff, where he had met Dr Emyr Wyn Jones, who he thought was very good. He had seen Mr Armon Ellis use his courtroom skills in the Town Hall in Denbigh, at a meeting of the Action Committee and then seen Dr (later Professor) David Jones, the CAMO in his own style demolish his argument. Lord Kenyon he thought a very clever man with a razor-like brain, who knew everyone, had a sense of humour, but poor eyesight – necessitating wearing thick glasses.

CHAPTER 9.1

MEMORIES OF NURSING
AND ANCILLARY STAFF

Ward Orderly – Mr D Buckley [1955-1981]

Huts

Mr D B was mainly on Hut A and Hut D between 1955 and 1965. Hut D was mostly for patients with orthopaedic problems and Hut A for chest, kidney and bladder affected illnesses. Each Hut was kept spotlessly clean as personal and ward hygiene was of great importance. Ward floors were thoroughly cleaned and polished and bathrooms, washrooms and toilets were scrubbed daily with pure **Lysol** disinfectant.

Patients were graded from being up for an hour, then 2, 4, 6, 8 hours and finally all day. Each patient had a stainless steel sputum mug with a flip-up lid on the locker next to the bed. Each day the amount of sputum in every sputum mug was measured in ounces and recorded in a book for each patient.

Sterile handkerchiefs were given to each patient every day and staff wearing mask, gown and gloves, using a bucket with a lid would collect soiled or used handkerchiefs which were then sent to the Hospital laundry for sterilisation. Other items of linen were counted, bagged and, using the same method of hygiene, were sent to the laundry to be sterilised. After each meal, crockery and cutlery were collected and taken to a designated room and put in metal crates and immersed in boiling water for 10-15 minutes, for sterilisation. Temperature, pulse and respiratory rates were recorded in a book each evening and treatment was PAS, INAH and Streptomycin.

Patients who were up all day were encouraged to take short walks and some of the walks around the hospital were graded for this purpose. Patients with Tuberculosis of the spine were put in plaster-casts, sometimes from neck to crutch, with provision made for toilet needs. Weather permitting, patients could be put out of doors in their beds through the French windows which were situated at the back of each bed.

At regular intervals each patient was interviewed and assessed by the Ward Doctor or Doctors in Sister's Office as to what progress they had made. Patients who were well enough were given opportunities to learn skills in the Occupational Therapy Department such as marquetry and making cotton duchesse sets. A recreation room near the Huts was available to play snooker, billiards and darts. Skittles could be played on the table in the centre of the Ward, or draughts or chess. Opportunities to see a film show or the entertainment in the staff dining room were available for patients who could walk to the room, but sometimes patients in their beds were wheeled down and then back to their Wards when the show was over.

Female patients were given domestic duties in cottages in the Hospital grounds specially provided for grading purposes. Patients were not allowed to visit the local Public Houses, but some inevitably broke the rules. Some patients would like a flutter on the horses, and a "runner" would collect slips of paper from each Ward daily and take them to the local Bookmakers!

Staff - 1955

Hut D
Sister McClure   - an Indian lady
Charge Nurse D R Jones - from Swansea

Staff Nurse J Farmer - a Lay Preacher in his spare time
Ward Orderlies - E Lloyd, Gwyn Hughes and
J I Evans
Night Orderlies - R Owen, Clem Hughes and J Carson
*[R Owen – Ward Orderly, Night Duty
(Hut D) had been employed as an
Estate Agent in Cheshire before
coming to Llangwyfan. A cheerful,
intelligent man who amused the
ladies at supper in the staff dining
room by telling their fortunes]*

Hut A

Sister K Penn *Née* Price - from Blaenau Ffestiniog
Staff Nurse A Morris - ex WWII Medical Orderly from
Bromborough
Staff Nurse Glenys
Parry *nee* Jones - of Pentrefoelas
Staff Nurse Eva Leyalais - of Wem, Shropshire
Nurse Auxiliary Esyllt
Williams - Edern
Ward Orderly T R Jones - originally from Rhos-y-Bol, Amlwch,
Ynys Môn *[who was a Seaman and
diagnosed with Tuberculosis after
going ashore in Australia. He com-
pleted his treatment in Llangwyfan]*
Ward Orderly D Buckley - Denbigh *[gained Part I of General
Nursing Council examination in
Anatomy, Physiology and Hygiene
whilst employed as a Student Nurse
in North Wales Hospital, Denbigh in
1953/4. Joined staff of Llangwyfan
as Ward Orderly in 1955]*

Ward Orderly
  R W Roberts - Ruthin, ex-WWII RAF
Ward Orderlies - C Rees, J E Jones

Hut B

Charge Nurse R
  Gallagher - later emigrated to Australia
Staff Nurse J Calclough - ex WWII Burma Veteran, originally
from Ellesmere Port
Ward Orderly E Hart - Denbigh
Ward Orderlies - C Hughes, Denbigh and J Carson,
Liverpool – ex service WWII. [*they
were warded on Hut D on night duty
and gave streptomycin injections on
the Ward before going off duty; but
later Ward Orderlies were not
allowed to give injections*]

Emyr Frances Roberts – Student Nurse [1949-1951]

Emyr was the youngest of 4 children of a Presbyterian Minister of Tegid Chapel, Bala, who was also a great pacifist.

He was interested in handwork and would have liked to have become an apprentice but his mother thought he should have the same college education as the rest of the family and he went to Cardiff in 1948 to read Chemistry, Physics and Mathematics at Intermediate grade. Because he was a Conscientious Objector he had to attend a Tribunal and was advised that if he didn't want to serve in the Armed Forces he had to work on the land or in the hospital service. He knew he didn't want to work on the land and decided to opt for hospital work and the Labour Exchange advised him there was work as an Orderly in Llangwyfan, where he was interviewed by Miss Morrison the Matron. She suggested to him, in view of the fact that he was a student, that he should become a Student Nurse, where the pay was slightly more than an Orderly's pay. What she didn't say was that he had to pay more for his accommodation in this grade. However, he accepted her suggestion and did 2 years training to get the BTA passing Parts I and II.

When he first got to Llangwyfan he lived in a cubicle in Lower Hut C (with a curtain in place of a door), but as he was paying more for this than an Orderly he complained and got a room in the Recreational Hall in Hut 4 where there were 4 rooms with bathroom en-suite occupied by Charlie Milne, Bob Deed and Student Nurse Jones. Orderlies paid 23 shillings a week whilst Student Nurses paid £202 per year and were entitled to better accommodation. No parties were held in the Recreation Hall when he was there and he has no recollection of the Boiler House next to it which heated the Huts.

Everything was different in Llangwyfan and though it was said to have 400 beds many wards were closed. He worked on Block 9 and the Huts and also three months in the Operating

Theatre with Charge Nurse Hall and Orderly Armstrong. He felt a very lowly member of staff and tried to avoid the medical staff's attention. He remembered Dr Hawkins, Medical Superintendent, who was followed by Dr Biagi, surgeons Mr Howell Hughes and Mr Hugh Reid, and Dr Ivor Lewis, the Anaesthetist who was Welsh speaking as was Mr Hughes.

The Huts were A, B, C and D and he worked in all of them. Sister Penn was in charge of A and Sister Brown of D, who was very friendly with Sister Murphy of Block 4. There were two Sisters Roberts and they were in charge of the Orthopaedic wards. During the 2 years of training there were blocks of teaching given by the Tutor, Sister Kate Williams, who was very good. They were taught to give drugs and injections such as Penicillin and Streptomycin, whereas Orderlies didn't do this. In Block 9 he nursed pre-operative and post-operative patients in a ward for 10 patients, also with 2 single rooms. He remembers nursing patients who had Thoracoplasty but not Lobectomy or Pneumonectomy. He had asked not to nurse children so he didn't go to Ward 8.

Charles Milne had been a Student Nurse before him and Bob Deedes followed him in this role. John Rees Jones who was another CO was an Orderly and later became a Teacher. He remembers Jean Griffiths of Denbigh and Kay Murphy as older girls who became Student Nurses. He also remembered Dr Gallagher.

He saw Dr Biagi doing Bronchoscopies in the Operating Theatre and also remembered Tonsillectomies being carried out but doesn't remember the Surgeon.

After he left Llangwyfan he trained in Salford College as a Sanitary Inspector, then Meat Inspector, then learnt about Atmospheric Pollution becoming an Environmental Health Officer. During one holiday he returned to Llangwyfan to work for 6 weeks.

His wife Marian had trained as a Midwife in Manchester and

they eventually, after several moves due to new jobs, settled in Llanfyllin moving to Portmadog after he retired. Marian had trained initially in the Royal Salop Infirmary and remembers patients with Tuberculosis being nursed in the open air in a separate ward.

Anwen Jones 1953-1956
[Cadet then BTA Training]

Anwen Jones arrived in Llangwyfan by bicycling from Derwen when she was 17½ years old to become a cadet on the Children's Ward – Block 8 – for six months; being too young then to start her nurse training. When she was 18 years old she started training under Sister Kate Williams, Nurse Tutor. She spent six weeks in the Preliminary Training School (PTS) then went on the Wards, returning to the PTS for blocks of training. After two years she passed the BTA examination. After they passed the BTA they were given £50, they called it danger money because of TB. One Nurse developed TB and didn't receive the £50 which she felt was very unfair. She remembers it as a sad place because there were so many young people there, but despite the fact that she was only there for 2½ years she has a good recollection of the happy time she spent there.

The Matron who interviewed her was Miss Morrison, a tall Scottish slim, smart lady who dressed well and who she liked. It was obvious that she was the Matron and in charge, but she didn't fear her. Her home whilst she was there was the first bungalow on the left, down from the Power House. Miss C B Roberts, the Assistant Matron, lived there, having her own sitting room, bedroom and bathroom and was a bit of a tyrant, later moving to Clatterbridge Hospital. There were also around 12 small rooms for student nurses.

Matron Morrison and later Matron Morris lived in the second bungalow. She has fond memories of the dances hosted by Dr

Biagi and Matron Morris which were very stylish. Miss Morris would invite local Denbigh dignitaries such as Police Inspectors and would appear resplendent in evening dress, whilst Dr Biagi wore a kilt and sporran. Everyone had to dress up and were able to take partners to the dance which were held between 8:00 pm and 12:00 midnight. She never saw any Surgeons at the dances, perhaps they weren't invited. [I was certainly never invited. – BO]

Mr Norman Roberts, the Orthopaedic Surgeon didn't visit often but when he did he visited female patients on Block 7, many in plaster beds; children in Block 8 and also men with Orthopaedic problems in Hut D. Charge Nurse R D Jones and Sister Maclure who was a dark Sister, petite and lovely were in charge in Hut D. She remembers Mr Roberts operating on the knee of a famous singer.

Mr Richard Doyle visited on a Friday, twice a month. He was a kidney man and because steak and kidney pie were on the menu on a Friday she would say she was a Catholic and ask for fish. Miss Coombs, as Deputy Matron, would serve dinners and she would ask "fish please". Miss Coombs didn't have much family life and lived for Llangwyfan. Mr Doyle would usually operate in the morning and leave at dinner time.

Mr Hugh Reid attended on Mondays and he carried out Pneumonectomies. Anwen developed Appendicitis and Mr Reid removed her appendix on August Bank Holiday Monday, and Dr D Rowlands gave her the anaesthetic.

Mr Ivor Lewis would operate on Thursday and his wife Dr Nancie Faux would give the anaesthetics. On Wednesday Mr Howell Hughes operated and his friend Dr Owen Ifor Lewis would anaesthetise. Dr Lewis was a comedian and he and Mr Hughes would banter-repartee. Charge Nurse Hall was very strict on Block 9 but, she said, there was no infection or clots, although one patient had a massive heart attack and died which was very unusual and upsetting for the rest of the hospital, as they were a community where everyone knew everything.. "Rudi", a German prisoner of war in Pool Park didn't speak much but taught her the theatre instruments involved as a Theatre Orderly in Llangwyfan. On a Sunday morning instruments were oiled, cleaned and sterilised by boiling. Many German nurses were recruited, with many remaining and marrying locally. She loved going to X-ray with patients and speaking to Miss Coop who married Mr Kellett Jones, the Dentist. There was a lot of respect for staff at that time, everyone being called by their title: Mr, Miss or Dr. There was a nice atmosphere and respect for the uniform and she never saw violence.

The staff she remembered were Dr Law, the Deputy Medical Superintendent who lived in Islwyn, who was a big man. He once found that she had allowed children to use Aluminium trays to slide down the incline between Block 7 and the pond over thick snow, but he did smile and agreed with her efforts to keep children amused and happy. She baby-sat for the Penrhyn Jones Family – Gruffydd and Lowri and said they were a very nice and lovely family. Dr Gallagher was pretty and nice. Dr Mayer gave nurses a rough time, but Sister Edwards, Ward Sister on Block 4, was ex-Army and her philosophy was that it was her responsibility to discipline nurses and so they were protected from Dr Mayer.

Dr Novak would show them the tattooed stamp on his forearm he was given as a prisoner in Auschwitz. He was completely bald and one Christmas was given a hair brush and comb as a present off the Christmas Tree. She said he was "chuffed" and pretended to use it on his scalp; joining in the fun.

Dr Munier was an Indian who worked on Block 9 and was very happy there looking after post operative patients. The Ward Sister was Sister Freda Jones, Wrexham trained, a large lady who was placid and cool who liked fun. In the early 1950's when Anwen was there the lay-out of the Blocks was as follows:-

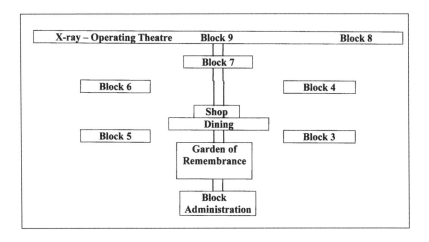

Block 3 – She thought was for special female patients and she never worked there. Sister Olwen Owen was in charge and she was called "Little O", a lovely lady. There were two Wards at the ends of this single storey building with four patients in each and in between about six single cubicles. It was a beautiful well run Ward with Dr Mayer looking after the patients and Dr Biagi often visiting them.

Blocks 4 and 6 – These were two storey buildings and seemed to her to be massive. All the patients upstairs were bed patients and as they improved they went downstairs to cubicles and were graded. All patients who were allowed to get up in Blocks 4 and 6, both two-storey buildings, had their meals downstairs. The bed-ridden patients' meals were carried upstairs and served by Sister. Those who had improved and were downstairs were expected to do their beds and keep the cubicles clean. After they had completed their grading they were allowed to go to the cottages. Sister in Charge of Block 4 was Sister Humphreys from Bala who later became Matron of Ruthin Hospital.

At the end of Block 4, upstairs, was Betty's corner. In the 8th

December 1939 House Sub-Committee Minutes there is reference to a gift by Mr Sidney Watkins of £200. in recognition of the unfailing care and attention of Dr Fenwick Jones and staff to his daughter Betty Lloyd Watkins. It had been proposed that this should be in Block 3, but after discussion it was agreed it should be an annexe upstairs in Block 4. Everything in this room was provided by Mr Watkins and there was also a plaque saying it was Betty's Corner.

Anwen didn't know until I told her that she was the sister of Ivor Watkins, the Denbigh Solicitor. She told me that she had nursed Mrs Watkins, their mother, during her last illness.

Huts

On the 8th September 1939 an Emergency Hospital Scheme came into effect. Patients were evacuated from Llangwyfan and sent home, 123 adult beds being vacated. However, shortly afterwards patients with TB were re-admitted. On the 8th December 1940 beds were unoccupied and it was decided that as the Thoracic Surgeons attending at Sully Hospital, South Wales had been deployed in the Armed Services that all patients needing Thoracic Surgery in Wales be admitted to Llangwyfan. It was agreed that 200 beds in Hutments were to be built in Llangwyfan for Service Men with Tuberculosis and war injuries. In 1940 the hutments were almost ready and although they were originally intended for war casualties it was proposed to use them immediately for the treatment of Tuberculosis in Service and Ex-Service Men. The pavilions were taken over one at a time and on the 10th January 1941 the first pavilion was opened. By April 76 beds were available and the appointment of a Handicraft Instructor was considered by the Sub-Committee.

When Anwen was there in the 1950's there were four huts. The top one was Hut B, housing 28-30 patients with Pulmonary TB being a well-run Ward under Charge Nurse Gallagher who was strict. He had two Staff Nurses and the rest of the staff were

Orderlies who were mostly ex-patients. Occupational Therapy was carried out in a separate room in Hut B.

Hut A was next with Sister Penn from Blaenau Ffestiniog who was marvellous at mothering a Ward of 30 young sexy men, but she was firm and had humour. After dark many of these patients walked down through the farm fields to the Kinmel Arms, Llandyrnog to keep out of Dr Biagi's way.

Hut D had less than 30 beds as it housed Orthopaedic patients on plaster beds which took far more room and were there a long time. It had French windows which opened so that patients could be wheeled outside. Charge Nurse D R Jones and Sister Maclure were here.

Hut C was opposite Hut D and an overflow Ward when other wards were being decorated in the hospital as the patients were moved there.

There was a room for an Eye Clinic in the Huts which Mr Harrington from Chester used. He was very tall and nice and removed a Meibomian Cyst from her eyelid. He came to the Hospital on request, not on a regular basis. She doesn't remember a Hut E.

The Dental room used by Mr Kellett Jones was on the same ward as the Dispensary and Laboratory and faced the valley. The Nurses from Block 4 ran this clinic.

She told me that there was no hassle, back chat or bullying in the Hospital. One job she didn't like doing was inspecting the cottages to see if they were clean. She felt Sister should have done it, as if they weren't kept clean the patients had to return to the Wards which they didn't like.

Some patients who were recovering had a relapse and were broken hearted and crying. These needed a lot of encouragement. The biggest depression, which occurred a lot, was when girls broke off their engagement to a young male patient. It occurred, but to a lesser extent, with young female patients when their fiancés left. There were a lot of patients from South Wales of both sexes. One girl was resistant to all the drugs used to treat her and her husband left her.

Concerts were held in the main hall to cheer up the patients and there were pictures (films) every Thursday night. Staff on duty had to watch when lights went out in case the patients left to meet boyfriends or girlfriends. Staff going out with patients was frowned upon. Dr Biagi didn't like it and staff could be dismissed.

Anwen learnt about life in Llangwyfan. One male patient with Osteomyelitis made sexual advances to an 18 year old male Orderly from Penmachno who didn't know such things could happen and had a terrible shock. The patient was told to leave immediately.

Anwen had been told that two female patients were not allowed to share a cubicle together. She thought it was because one was Mantoux positive and the other negative. She asked later what the reason was and was told that they were lesbians. She didn't know anything about lesbians and when she learnt the reason was afraid of them. At her age she could cope with TB positive patients, but not with this homosexuality.

'Pigeon Post' between patients was allowed by staff and if a friend was in Block 9 and they were "on grades" they were allowed to take the grade past the window to see their friend. Sister Freda Jones would allow this and also allow them to talk through the window. She said the food was excellent with "full" everything: full breakfast, full lunch, full dinner. The main Chef was Charlie Griffiths. There were a lot of Conscientious Objectors there. One who was a Minister of Religion worked in the kitchen and another who was a Chemistry Student was utilised in the Pathology Laboratory to help Mr Richards. Mr Richards was lame and wore a big wedge shoe. He was a pleasant, big Welshman and spoke Welsh to everyone he knew who spoke the language. She used to go to the Laboratory to take sputum specimens for analysis once a month. There had to be three negative specimens before surgery was carried out and consequently patients had at least a 3 month wait.

The "Garden of Remembrance" was in the shape of a 50p piece and had very nice wicker furniture and French doors on both sides. People waited there before being interviewed. It was situated between Administration and the Dining Hall and was in remembrance of someone.

The bust of Edward VII had a plaque on it and also there was a plaque in Betty's corner.

Anwen told me that the Administrator of Llangwyfan, Miss Salt, "was a right tyrant". If the wages were wrong "God help us". Other staff have told me she was a good Administrator. The Sisters lived in Cwyfan and the Porter, Mr Craig, lived in the main lodge.

Anwen though said that the Tennis Courts in front of the main entrance were beautiful, the gardens were lovely and the pond.

The shop behind the Dining Room was started when she was there. Charlie Wills had a shop in Llandyrnog and would take cigarettes and sweets around the wards on a trolley. She called cigarettes "fags". He had a stand in the car park on Saturday and Sunday when there were a lot of visitors. He was very good with patients who made him wealthy, but he wasn't a grabber. Cae Lloi buses from Pwllheli would bring visitors at the weekend, always being full.

She took adult patients on trips to, for example, Denbigh Moors when she was in PTS. They weren't allowed to go into cafés but would take hampers of food.

The Deputy Medical Superintendent lived in the new Plas Llangwyfan. Dr Mayer and Dr Novak lived in the main block upstairs where there was also a Nurses Sick block. The Nurses were looked after by Dr Biagi.

Anwen's sister had trained for her SRN in the Middlesex Hospital and Tooting Grove Fever Hospital and was in London through the war. The Middlesex was bombed when she was on night duty and she fell through the floor, fracturing her elbow. Afterwards, she wanted peace and quiet and applied for a post in Llangwyfan in 1945-46 becoming Theatre Sister and completing the BTA in a year. She was living in Derwen with her parents and would cycle to Llangwyfan thoroughly enjoying the countryside and the slower pace of life. Llangwyfan was full of Army patients and post-Japanese war Servicemen and Prisoners of War who needed to be fed. The food was excellent and she told me that her brother worked in a Butcher's Shop in Ruthin and his recollection is of preparing 600 lb of sausages every week for Llangwyfan.

Anwen remembered the time that 20-25 girls were infected with Tuberculosis in the carpet factory called Old Hall, in Blaenau Ffestiniog. Some were admitted to the Druid in Llangefni, some to Bryn Seiont, Blaenau Ffestiniog and the worst infected came to Llangwyfan – some in Block 4 and others in Block 6.

To get to the Pathology Laboratory, Dispensary and Little PTS room you entered the building through the same door. Next-door to the PTS room in the same building was a Recreation Room which had a piano where patients could go. She thought religious services were also held in this room, although she doesn't remember attending. She told me there was a lack of visiting by Clergy. The Reverend Hywel Jones of Capel y Dyffryn, Llandyrnog visited patients but she didn't see any Catholic or Church in Wales Clergy and doesn't remember any Sunday Services. She would either work Sunday morning and then have the rest of the day off or have the morning off and work in the afternoon. The Nurses working in the mornings would do a bed pan round before going off duty, but one Sunday when she came on duty the male patients rang the bell to say they hadn't had the bed pans. She wasn't at all pleased but handed them out and left the ward. They then rang the bell to say they had finished and she could collect them. When she picked the first bed pan up it was very heavy – they had put bricks in the bed pans! They were waiting for her to pull her leg and play tricks on her but they all had a great laugh.

The school was between X-ray and the huts. Sister Holden was the Night Superintendent. She enjoyed her time in Llangwyfan with Block 8 being the only block where she wasn't happy. One member of staff in Block 8 was very nice but the other was not and this one became friendly with Senior Nursing Staff so one had to be careful of her.

Sister Ross Jones
[Wife of Charge Nurse D B Jones]

She trained as a Nurse (SRN) in Llandudno with part of her training taking place in Llangwyfan, which she enjoyed. She and her friend Mari who later married Charge Nurse Eddie Edwards, decided to go to Papworth Hospital, Cambridge to work not realising until they got there how different it would be. They took fright and decided to leave and were offered Staff Nurse posts in Llangwyfan by Miss B Morris, the Matron. She was a Sister on Block 9 and 5 until 1964, when she left to have her family. She returned as a Staff Nurse on nights part time until she was able to take a whole time appointment, when she became a Sister and worked on nights until the Hospital closed.

She enjoyed working in Llangwyfan and told me most people were terrified of Ivor Lewis. He appeared on Block 9 one day and asked her for a "File Cyffredin" – a common file. She had no idea what he wanted but produced a patient's file – not what he wanted at all. He kept saying "File Cyffredin" and Tom Jones, the Orderly on the Ward, came to her rescue, went out of the Ward and returned with a Carpenter's file – just what he needed to file the end of a plastic syringe to fit an adapter for a certain procedure. Then he told them to keep the plastic syringe in case

123

he needed to use it again. On one occasion, he left his wife behind and went home forgetting she was in Llangwyfan with him, and had to return for her.

She said that towards the end it was very difficult to recruit staff. She had an Auxiliary Nurse and a Domestic, but had to do everything else herself.

Jean Richards (née Brown) SRN, Ward Sister from 1953-1956 and her husband John Richards, Laboratory Technician

Jean Brown was born and brought up in Mynydd Isa, Flintshire and gained her SRN in the Wrexham War Memorial Hospital. She then did Part I of Midwifery Training in the Queen Charlotte's Hospital, London in 1952 for six months, and Part II in the Training Centre in Middleton Square in London for six months. Following which, she returned as a Staff Midwife to Groes Newydd, Maelor. Two friends she made in Wrexham developed Tuberculosis and she decided to apply to work in Llangwyfan, and was interviewed for a Staff Nurse post by Miss Morrison. However, when she went around the Hospital she found girls who were Sisters not as qualified or experienced as she was and she wrote to Matron to ask if she could be graded as 'Sister'. This was agreed and she worked in Llangwyfan from November 1953 for two years. When she left she worked for six months in Mancot Maternity Hospital, married John and they moved to Liverpool where she worked in various posts as a Midwife, School Health Visitor and Occupational Health Sister until her son, Sion, was born in 1972. He became a Scientist and works on the health and dietary problems of animals.

Jean was the Sister running Blocks 4 and 5, both being female wards, which at that time were very busy. Block 4 was mainly for bedridden patients, many of whom had postural retention. This

124

was being used extensively, a long padded board being used to make a splint by the Physiotherapist and passed from the head to the foot of the bed to which it was attached. The patient was nursed lying on the diseased side to rest it, and remained in this position, not being allowed out of bed or to sit up. They were able to manage to eat and toilet themselves, although help was available if it was needed.

There were approximately 60 beds on Blocks 4 and 5; 30 upstairs and 15 downstairs in Block 4, and 15 beds in Block 5. Most of the patients were young women, some of whom came from the small Tuberculosis Hospitals in Wales as there was a waiting list to get into Llangwyfan. Some patients went on to have AP and PP refills or surgery such as Thoracoplasty and Lobectomies which were carried out by Mr Howell Hughes, Mr Hugh Reid or Mr Ivor Lewis who also undertook Bronchoscopies. With improved treatment of Tuberculosis the number of patients needing admission declined. She thought the food was good and couldn't remember any problems with drugs. She worked almost entirely with Dr Mayer which she enjoyed. If there were problem patients they had case conferences with the Surgeon and Dr Biagi and his staff to decide future progress. On one occasion when Jean had first joined the staff, Dr Mayer was explaining to her how to carry out a PP refill on a Nursing Tutor and the importance of the correct position for the needle, when the Tutor said "if it is in the wrong place the patient dies"!

She shared her birthday with Dr Mayer who took her on a trip in her car to Denbigh Moors on their birthday, then returning to have a meal in the Bull Hotel, Denbigh. Dr Mayer was very regal, but later was admitted to Clatterbridge for treatment and Jean went to see her there and saw a very frail lady. She thought that Dr Mayer had family in Germany who sent her Christmas presents, but she never heard of her husband.

She never worked with Dr Gallagher who covered Block 6 and Hut D.

Jean remembered Sisters Maclure, Bella Griffiths, Penn, Little "O" and Humphreys when she was there. Sister Humphreys later became Matron of Ruthin Hospital. Also Sister Freda Jones was in charge of Block 9. Sister Bella Griffiths got married on an Open Day in Llangwyfan. Her nursing friends were allowed to go to the wedding but not to the reception, and therefore a mini reception was provided for them in the Chapel House before they returned to Llangwyfan. Dr Brew, a House Officer and who was Catholic, refused to take them to the wedding but Dr Novak readily agreed. Dr Novak was in Llangwyfan the whole time that she and John (who became her husband) were there. He was a Registrar, working mainly in the huts, a good Doctor and a very nice person. Everyone valued him as a friend.

Block 5 was for Graders, some of whom went on to the cottages. They were graded by Dr Mayer every one or two weeks, and seen individually to be assessed. They were given little jobs to carry out after that.

Jean thought Llangwyfan a very happy establishment, although visiting could be difficult for relatives who might have long distances to travel.

Her late husband **John Richards (1920-2004)** was from Tŷ'n Coed, Lledrod, Cardiganshire. He was born on the 7th December 1920. His father died when he was 11 years old and he helped his mother to run the farm, with the assistance of a farm labourer. He shared a bed with another boy who helped them and Jean thought he developed Tuberculosis from this contact. However, John had Tuberculosis of the hip and this could have been due to the bovine type although no-one else in the family had contracted it. His brother Tommie was still in school and in the late 1930's John was admitted to Llangwyfan and became a patient on Block 6. John was nursed on a frame for two years and went home in a Thomas' Splint. He told Jean that the Porters were all very kind to the male patients on Block 6 as before they went off duty they would go around the ward to see if anyone wanted anything from outside, such as from Denbigh. Because visitors were a rarity for many, this was considered a great kindness which John never forgot. While he was in Llangwyfan he completed his A-levels.

His mother visited him once a month and was fortunate that as she didn't own a car, District Nurse Price from Llanilar would drive her to Llangwyfan to see him. I was told District Nurse Price was a marvellous woman and that she did this in a voluntary capacity when she was off duty. There were buses that brought visitors to Llangwyfan once a month, from a long way off, many stayed in bed and breakfast establishments in Llandyrnog.

When John returned home to Lledrod he had a stiff hip and couldn't ride a horse which was a necessity at that time in order to see their stock; so he went to work in a Veterinary Laboratory in Aberystwyth. He then attended the University College, following which he went to Coventry and Warwick to work in a Medical Laboratory, where he passed his examinations to qualify as a Laboratory Technician. In 1953 he returned to Llangwyfan to open the Laboratory under guidance of Dr T Alban Lloyd. From notes made on the early days of the Sanatorium in 1922 the Pathology Laboratory was a mobile hut arrangement situated at the rear of the Isolation Block, which later became a residence for the Pathology Technician. When the new Light Department was opened in 1929 it included a Laboratory and Dispensary. By the 1950's a new building next to Blocks 8 and 9 housed the Laboratory. It was spacious and he was busy all day with plenty of work to be done. Jean would take specimens to the Laboratory.

They both left and married in 1956. John was Best Man to Charge Nurse Glyn Jones, and was also a helper with the Scouts in Llangwyfan. After their marriage she and John lived on the Wirral as he worked in Heswell in the Royal Liverpool Children's Hospital from 1961 to 1985. They then returned to live in

Bodfari. John died on the 3rd March 2004. He did a radio interview with Hywel Gwynfryn about Llangwyfan.

Mary Royles SRN, BTA
Staff Nurse, Night Sister [1953-1980]

Mary Royles qualified as a State Registered Nurse (SRN) from Sefton General Hospital, Liverpool in the early 1950's and after working there for twelve months got a post as a Staff Nurse in Llangwyfan, starting at the end of 1953. She married Mossie who was Head Chef at Llangwyfan in 1955 and after leaving to have her family of two daughters returned in 1961 as a Night Sister, staying until it closed in 1980. The biggest change which had occurred during her absence was that the number of patients with Tuberculosis had gone down due to treatment with Streptomycin and the plaster casts had gone. Patients normally stayed approximately 2 years.

She was interviewed for her first appointment by Miss Kathryn Roberts, the Deputy Matron, who came from Pwllheli and was very strict. The Matron, Miss Morrison, had just retired and was described as a plump little Scottish lady. She was followed by Miss Blodwen Morris as Matron.

She stayed for a time in Hut 1 of the lower Huts. The Hut had been planned to contain rooms and she had a small room which had a door, but didn't like it at first because it was next to the mortuary and she said she would have refused it if she'd realised this beforehand. There were about 10-20 female staff in this Hut.

Hut 2 was for female orderlies, about 10-20 in number. A small kitchen was provided but not used because they all went to the dining room where the food was good. Hut 3 had males of various grades, again divided into rooms with 3 walls, but no door. The fourth wall being a moveable curtain. Hut 4 was the recreation room and they all lived in this large open heated area with seating which had a table tennis table, billiards and a record

Night Sisters Group – *Left to right:* Molly Edwards, Myra Andrews, Dorothy Ansell Jones, Winnie Wilson, Linda Davies, SEN, Annie Williams (Auxilliary), Mary Royles (*centre*), Sally Jones, Haf Watson

Tecwyn Jones, Orderly

Fancy Dress – Eta Harnell and Mossie Royles "Nighty Night" 1977

Night Staff – Jan 1977: *Standing left to right:* Sr Sally Jones, Ch/N Glyn Jones.
Sitting: Srs Winnie Wilson, Mary Royles, Haf Watson

Shop 1954 – Sister Mary Royles with 2 patients

Margaret Joy Griffiths (left) and Pat.
The Power House is behind them and Staff Bungalows on their left

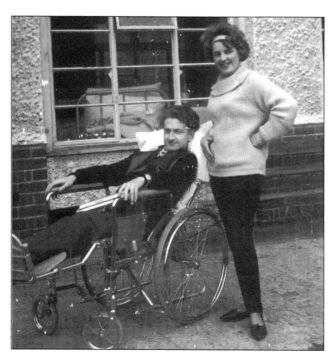

Dwelyn Jones
in wheelchair
with Ross
Jones

Outside Block 9
Mari Edwards, Sam, Ross Jones, B. Cowlishaw

Mrs Breeze, Hospital Almoner as a Wales supporter and David Buckley as a makeshift Sheik of Araby

Esyllt Williams (N/Aux), D Buckley (Orderly), E Legallais S/N,
Edna (student Nurse) - 1956

Off for a day's golf – 1980: Eric Doolan, David Buckley,
Ch/Nurse Mike Jones

Miss Margaret Rich and Miss J G Hughes

Tel. No. RHYL 1581 & 1582.

Clwyd and Deeside Hospital Management Committee.

WILLIAM ROBERTS, F.H.A.
GROUP SECRETARY AND SUPPLIES OFFICER

Our Ref 178/7/8

"RHIANFA."

RUSSELL ROAD,

K. W. THOMAS, A.I.M.T.A., A.C.W.A., A.H.A.
FINANCE OFFICER.

RHYL.

10th January 1961

Miss J.G. Hughes,
4 Cheltenham Avenue,
RHYL.

Dear Madam,

Llangwyfan Hospital, Near Denbigh.
Appointment of Senior Occupational Therapist.

I refer to your application and subsequent interview by the
Physician Superintendent (Dr. R.W. Biagi) and now write to confirm the
offer to you of the above appointment. The scale of salary prescribed
for a whole-time Senior Occupational Therapist is £580 x £25(4) -
£680 x £30 - £710 maximum. In your case as you have not had three
years experience since qualifying, the minimum of the scale is to be
abated by one increment for each year, or part of a year short of the
required three years. Your commencing salary will therefore be £530
per annum. Increments on the scale are payable on completion of each
year's experience until qualified for the normal minimum and this date
will be regarded as your incremental date.

The appointment will be subject to the conditions of service
prescribed from time to time by the Professional and Technical Council
"A" of the Whitley Councils for the Health Services, the Health Service
(Superannuation) Regulations, the National Insurance Acts and to one
month's notice on either side.

If the offer of the appointment is acceptable, will you please
confirm your acceptance and at the same time let me know the earliest
date upon which you will be able to commence duties.

Yours faithfully,

Group Secretary.

Letter of Appointment – Senior Occupational Appointment

Staff Xmas/Fancy
Dress Party 1977:
Mary Royles,
Linda Davies,
Annie Williams,
Ross Jones,
Sr Winnie Wilson

Fancy Dress – 1950s.
Left to right: Mary Terzo, Betty ?, Gwen Williams, Mackie Sisters, Betty Griffiths, ?,
?, Peggy Lloyd, ?, Marian Baxter, Mary Payne

Teulu Llyndir

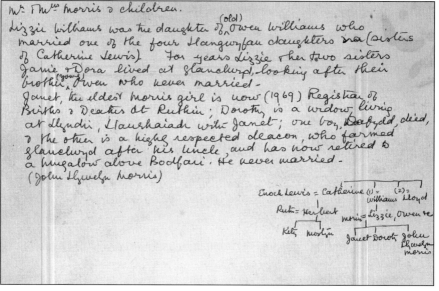

Reverse of the above photograph – written by Kitty Idwal Jones

MP guest of League of Friends at AGM.
Left ro right: Mr Lloyd (Matron), Dr Biagi (Med. Supt),
Mrs Norbury (Vice-chair), Mr Emrys Roberts (Chair), Miss Morris (Sec.),
Dafydd Ellis Thomas (MP), ?

Ann Clwyd as guest speaker – AGM League of Friends

An Appeal
to the
people of
Uwchaled

AN APPEAL

Since 1948, all necessary hospital treatment has been provided by the National Health Services but there is ample scope for voluntary effort in the provision of amenities—more especially in "long stay" hospitals such as Sanatoria.

Many areas in North Wales have helped generously during the last few years and the gifts of television sets and other amenities have been very welcome and appreciated—such generosity and thoughtfulness have been a great help to patients to while away the long weary hours.

At the last meeting of the local Committee of the Llanrwst National Eisteddfod 1951, it was reported that there still remained a surplus of £39 for distribution and it was unanimously agreed to hand this sum over as a nucleus to form a local fund to meet one of the pressing needs of Llangwyfan Hospital—a piano for the recreation of the patients and staff.

It was decided to make an appeal to the people of Uwchaled to raise a fund sufficient to purchase an instrument which would be worthy of the area and to enlist the co-operation of the Churches in the collection of subscriptions up to August 27th. next.

It is hoped that everybody will take advantage of this opportunity of showing in a practical and generous way their appreciation of the good work of Llangwyfan Hospital, not only in our own localities but for the whole of Wales.

EIFION ROBERTS, CEFNBRITH,
Chairman.

EMRYS JONES, LLANGWM,
Secretary.

I. W. ROBERTS, CERRIGYDRUDION,
Treasurer.

JULY 1956.

APÊL

Er bod darpariaeth ar gyfer pob triniaeth feddygol o dan y Ddeddf Iechyd, mae lle ac angen am gynorthwy wirfoddol i ddarparu cysuron ychwanegol yn arbennig ar gyfer cleifion sydd yn gorfod aros am hir amser mewn ysbyty debyg i Sanatorium.

Y mae rhai ardaloedd eisioes wedi cyfranu yn hael tuag at setiau teledu, etc. i wahanol ysbytai a gwerthfawrogir eu meddwlgarwch a'i caredigrwydd i dorri ar unffurfiaeth y "dyddiau blin."

Mewn cyfarfod o Bwyllgor Lleol Eisteddfod Genedlaethol Llanrwst, 1951, hysbyswyd fod gweddill o £39 mewn llaw, wedi ei drosglwyddo yn ôl i'r ardal i'w ddosbarthu. Ar ôl ystyriaeth fanwl, penderfynwyd defnyddio yr arian i ffurfio cnewyllyn i gronfa i gyfarfod ag un o anghenion mwyaf Ysbyty Llangwyfan, sef piano at wasanaeth y cleifion a'r gweinyddesau.

Er mwyn sicrhau offeryn teilwng o Uwchaled, penderfynwyd apelio at drigolion yr ardal am gynorthwy sylweddol a threfnwyd i ofyn i'r Eglwysi drefnu i dderbyn tanysgrifiadau o hyn i Awst 27, 1956.

Mawr hyderwn y bydd cefnogaeth gyffredinol a pharod i'r apêl yma, er mwyn manteisio ar y cyfle i ddatgan gwerthfawrogiad mewn dull ymarferol o'r gwaith da a wneir gan Llangwyfan, nid yn unig i'n ardaloedd ni ond hefyd i Gymru gyfan.

EIFION ROBERTS, CEFNBRITH,
Cadeirydd.

EMRYS JONES, LLANGWM,
Ysgrifennydd.

I. W. ROBERTS, CERRIGYDRUDION,
Trysorydd.

GORFFENNAF 1956.

Presentation of chairs from Uwchaled League of Friends— 1963.
Peter Roys (Group Sec.), Blodwen Morris (Matron), David Jones (Hospital Sec.),
Mrs Claudia Davies (Vice-chair League), Clifford Robinson (House Committee + HMC),
Mrs Suzy Hughes (Chairman of League), Mrs. K. W. Parry (Sec. of League of Friends), Emrys Roberts

League of Friends Supper 1979

Lily the Pink – Fancy Dress Party January 1969 with Legend
Norma Wayne is "Lily the Pink" wearing the pink coat. Mrs Davies (sitting) was the
Compound. Big Ears (standing behind was Raymond Davies, Orderly).

In the 1960's Lydia Pinkham's medicinal compound was a pop song in America,
but when it came to this country it was changed to Lily the Pink as the BBC would
not play the original version.

The original Lily was Lydia Estes Pinkham (1819-1883), a resident of
Massachusetts. In the 19th Century potent remedies saved the expense of
consulting the doctor. Pinkham made up some herbal concoctions, the most
successful of which was Lydia E Pinkham's Vegetable Compound, marketed from
1875. It was used for "women's complaints" – period pains and menopausal
symptoms. The mixture contained 6 herbs dissolved in 18% alcohol.

Sr Morfydd Jones Hut B and staff outside in the grounds
From left: Ernie Hart (Orderly), Dr Hussain (House Officer), Tecwyn Hywel Davies
(Orderly), Kathleen Williams (Auxiliary), Sr Morfydd Jones, Miss Wynne (Domestic)

S/N Sally Jones and Sister Morfydd Jones – buttercups in the lawn

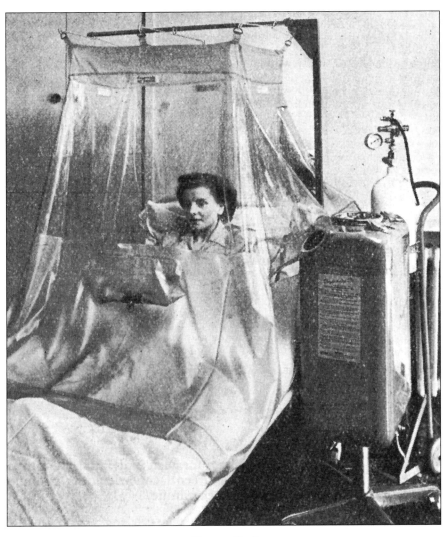

Oxygen Tent

Demonstration in the kitchen

Enid Humphreys cutting sausages 1955

Llangwyfan
Space
Rocket

Anita Groome
standing on the
wooden bridge
near the pond

Dr Novak with young women patients outside Block 4

Anita second
from left –
started Grades

Young female Graders outside Block 4

Anita in the middle – in the orchard

In the Orchard
having fun

Below:
Letter from
Dr Biagi to
Dr Davies

Clwyd and Deeside Hospital Management Committee.

Telegrams—LLANGWYFAN HOSPITAL, DENBIGH
Railway Station—DENBIGH, 4½ miles
Telephone—LLANDYRNOG 202

LLANGWYFAN HOSPITAL,

Near DENBIGH

RWB/AIW

19th January 1961

Dear Dr.Davies,

Thank you for your letter of 12.1.61. I am enclosing one further account for rose bushes which will complete our request to you in this matter.

As I said before, it has been tremendously helpful being able to call on this fund to complete the needs for our gardens. Without doubt the Management Committee are extremely good to us in every way, but inevitably they tend to cut down the requirements to the bare minimum and often, especially in the gardens, the effect is spoilt to a great extent by this economy. The funds that have been supplied by you make all the difference, and we are indeed grateful. If I could leave the remaining sum available until the need arises I should be pleased. We can always spend it just now, but so often when spent rather hurriedly the best use is not made of the money.

Kindest regards,

William Biagi

Ivor Davies
Iron Afallen
CERRIGYDRUIDION
Corwen.

Doctors and Nurses Dining room attendants – 1962.
Back row, left to right: Eirwen Lloyd, Edith Roberts, Jean (nee Lloyd).
Front row: Gwyneth Simmons, Lorraine (nee Lloyd), Margaret Baxter

Kitchen Staff.
Back row: Mossie Royles, Charlie Griffiths, ?, Edith, Margaret.
Front row: ?, ? Sullivan, Stella Williams, ?.

On stage – 1950:
Background: Matron Blodwen Morris. Foreground: Dr William Biagi
Front row – second from left: Edith Roberts

Cliff Rees,
Orderly and
Rosalind,
Aux Nurse
who were
married in
1962

This picture and the following are from the Len Jones collection 1936-1939.
Len is standing in the middle outside Block 8 awaiting Rt Hon Walter Elliott (1939)
to cut the first turf for the huts

Yn sefyll, o'r chwith:
? Taylor
bachgen o Wrecsam.
Len Jones.
?
un o Langefni, wyr i archddeuwydd
Eisteddfod Môn.

Yn disgwyl ymweliad Sir Walter Elliott,
Gweinidog Iechyd i dorri'r dywarchen
gyntaf yr "huts" 1939.

The reverse side of the above photograph

An aerial view of Llangwyfan, showing church, huts and bungalows

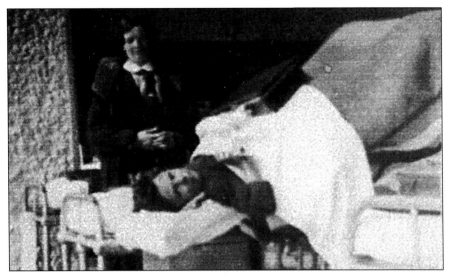

Len in Gobowen bed, with Miss Chamberlain

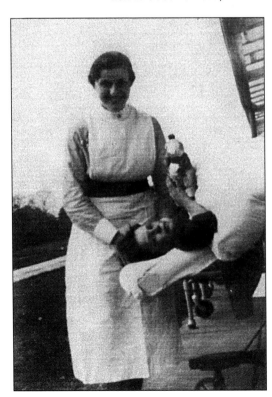

Sister Holden with Len

Children in their beds on the veranda

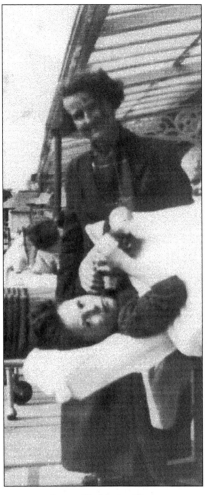

Len with his mother

Len with his father

Len on the veranda, walking and getting better

Boy passes school exam. in hospital

WHEN Harold John Morris, of Glynceiriog, wanted to sit for the annual examinations giving admission to various county schools in Denbighshire, an education official had to go to the North Wales Sanatorium School, Llangwyfan.

Harold, who has been ill for more than three years, is due to leave the sanatorium soon. He gained 216 marks in the test. won a special place for Llangollen County School. He hopes to go there in September.

the Prince Edward War Memorial Hospital, it was announced last night. Mr Elliot will be invited also to

A school success for Harold John Morris

A view of the children's block

Block 6 and Block 7

Children on the beach in Rhyl with Sister Holden and Miss Price, teacher

Len on his way home in Conwy

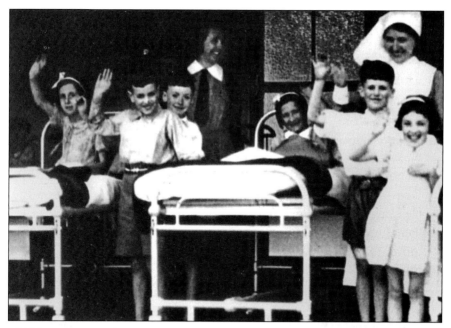

Children waving at Rt Hon W Elliott, MP. Miss Price and Sister Holden in the back
with Len in front of Sister

o'r chwith:
?, Taylor, Llangathri, Miss Price (athrawes), ?,
Len Jones, Sister Holden, ?.

Yn disgwyl Sir Walter Elliott ar ôl iddo
domi'r dywarchen gyntaf, 1939.

Stills o "negatives" film newsreel o'r
ymweliad. Tynnyd gan John Hughes,
Projectionist Palladium, Pwllheli (cyfaill
teulud).

The reverse of the above photograph

player. There were no parties at first, but later I was told there were very good parties held there.

These Huts were on the right of the lane that went down to the farm. Lower down the lane and past the new farm house, on the left side were 4 staff houses. Mary and Mossie lived in number 3 Tanyffordd after they started a family. She remembers Charge Nurse Arthur Hall who worked in the Operating Theatre, living in number 1 until 1959 and he was followed by Charge Nurse Glyn Jones. Staff Nurse Bobbie Deed lived at number 2 and Gordon Holmes in number 4. They formed a very friendly community with the children playing well together without the aid of television to amuse them. She told me that she made a mistake in sending their children to Llandyrnog school. She thought it would be a Welsh school as she was Welsh speaking, but found out too late that it was an English school and the Welsh school was at Gellifor. Gellifor pupils later went to Ruthin Comprehensive school whilst Llandyrnog pupils went to Denbigh. Later the Royles moved to live in Denbigh.

She remembers Mr Edwards farming Llangwyfan, but did not get to know him. Later, Clwyd and Eleanor Hughes lived in the farm house and their children played with the Tanyffordd children for although at that time the farm was not part of the hospital, they were still in the same community.

Between the farm buildings and the huts there was a small boiler house to provide heating for the huts and this had to be stoked twice a day by the hospital staff – Emlyn Bach was a stoker, and Mr Brierly an engineer. They would stoke with anthracite which had been tipped nearby, the first stoke being at 4:30 am and on their way back they would wake Mossie Royles who had to be on duty in the kitchen at 6:00 am.

When they moved to live in Denbigh she was able to avail herself of the hospital transport which brought the night staff into work every night and also took them home when they finished duty in the morning. This was a big grey bus which was kept in the garage next to the mortuary and driven by Jack Jones, the hospital chauffeur, or by Hughie Evans, Groes Efa. This was provided by Clwyd and Deeside HMC.

Sister Holden was the Night Superintendent from 1950-1958/9 and following her were:

    Rex Gallagher
    John Best
    John Griffin
    Glyn Jones
    Winnie Wilson

The Night Sisters were:
    Vera Yurgensen
    Myra Andrews
    Gladys Myddleton
    Olive Roberts
    Mary Royles   }
    Molly Edwards }
    Sally Jones   } were there until Llangwyfan closed
    D Ansell Jones }
    Hâf Watson   }

There were around 400 beds in use and covered by two Sisters at night. They alternated their duties – one covering female patients and the other the male patients and the huts, which had 30 patients each. This entailed a lot of walking and they were kept busy all night. Female patients could be covered along covered ways between 3, 4, 7, 8 and 9. Top Huts A, B, C and D were all male Nightingale Wards with the bottom doors never being shut and cows heads could appear over the top of the hedge in the day and look in. Occasionally there would be indications that there were prowlers outside and the Police were contacted and asked to investigate, but they would arrive with sirens blazing which would drive any intruders away. Other funny incidents, but frightening, was the noise created by mating badgers, sounding like shouting and screaming. There was a sett near the Church and mating would take place on the path leading to Vron Yw.

When she arrived on duty she would leave her outdoor clothes in a locker, in a room over the main kitchen, then report to Matron who told the staff where to go. Three official ward rounds per night were carried out and if an emergency occurred this was reported by telephone to Block 9, which was their base for the night. When Sister did her Ward round she would carry the drug box with her which was locked, and the drug book, and she would dispense drugs on the wards if they were needed and record in the book. At the end of the ward round the two Sisters would check the drugs returned. A gradual shut down of the huts took place as the number of patients declined over the years.

Patients from the North Wales Hospital were in Hut D. There were no mental health Night Sisters and they had to provide cover for the Denbigh Nurses. The Night Superintendent from Denbigh, Charge Nurse Gwilym Hughes, would visit two to three times a week. She remembered patients having falls and she had to witness deaths, but didn't otherwise get involved. These patients were mobile and dressed every day, but they rambled and were confused. The Pulmonary Function Room was opposite Hut A; the Occupational Therapy Room was opposite Hut B.

The Pharmacy was near the Power House between Block 8 and the Dispensary. Occasionally, patients needed to be sectioned under the Mental Health Act and were certified by two doctors – one from the North Wales Hospital and the other Llangwyfan, usually Dr Biagi. Two ambulance men would attend to take the patient to Denbigh. She said the cause for this was electrolyte imbalance or oxygen toxicity as oxygen levels were not carried out routinely then. She does not remember iron lungs in Llangwyfan, nor did she ever see patients being ventilated at night.

There would be 2 to 3 admissions at night per week, mostly readmissions because of chest problems, bronchospasm or haemoptysis – she saw three who died of this. The General Practitioner would ring to speak to her and she would get permission from the doctor on call to admit the patient. Some patients would need quite a bit of time to admit them and the doctor would come to examine and treat them. At night patients were mostly admitted to Ward 9, but occasionally would be admitted to whichever block had an empty bed. The resident doctor would live on the first floor of the administration block which meant there was always a doctor on call every night in the hospital.

Oxygen tents were in frequent use and there could be up to four in use in one room. These were very noisy in the middle of the night in Block 9, 6, 4 and 3. First the tent was erected from the flat pack where it was housed. The plastic sheets had lots of metal hooks and zips for closure, making nursing cumbersome. A stand with a container for ice was applied to the back of the frame and filling this with ice to cool the oxygen was noisy.

Staff would go to the freezer in the main kitchen to fetch the ice, this was then chopped into appropriate pieces which were then fed into the container. Most patients were understanding of the need to do this and did not complain of the noise created when the container had to be kept filled. Oxygen entered the tent from large cylinders which were brought to the ward and stored behind Block 9 when not in use. Orderlies usually helped to transport the cylinders but if they were busy the boiler man helped.

The tent was first saturated with oxygen at 12 litres per minute, then brought down to eight litres per minute and then the patient was put in the tent. Most staff were not trained to do this work and it was Sister's role to make sure the procedure was correct.

Night Staff worked from 8:00 pm to 7:30 am with an hour for dinner which could be taken between 11:00 pm and 12:00

midnight, or from 12:00 midnight to 1:00 am together with a half hour for tea, and for these they went to the dining room. In the 1960's there was a separate building of a shop near the back kitchen door which sold basic hygiene toiletries. Latterly The League of Friends kept their trolleys there. There was also a garden of remembrance between the administration building and the kitchen, which looked like a conservatory. It had pillars and was glassed in with tables and basket work chairs which was popular with staff after dinner. Flowers which were given to the hospital were put in there creating a beautiful and tranquil area. Both these buildings have gone.

She pointed out to me in a photograph of Miss Blodwen Morris' retirement party, Greta Jones who was a domestic in the kitchen. Her son, Tecwyn Jones was an Orderly on Night Duty – the longest serving Orderly. A Denbigh lad, he had served in the Royal Navy before coming to Llangwyfan where he was remembered with affection, following his early death. He was a quiet all-rounder who would mix with anyone and was courteous. He helped in the Operating Theatre and was good with genitourinary patients. He moved to Glan Clwyd to work in the Theatre and trained as a Theatre Technician. Unfortunately, he developed cardiac problems and died suddenly at home. She also told me that Nurse Olwen Hughes who appeared in a photograph with Sister Bassett was a very good nurse who had worked in Glan y Wern Hall, Llandyrnog; a mansion converted to a hospital during the war.

Clwyd and Deeside HMC had provided transport to take staff to Rhyl twice a week. If they paid for transport the staff could claim it back because they were looking after Tuberculosis patients. If they came back on ordinary transport to Denbigh they were met to take them to Llangwyfan. When the weather was bad they walked from Denbigh to Llangwyfan. Winnie Wilson remembers staying a night in Llangwyfan and walking home the next day in 1964.

Addendum by Buddug Owen

There are two types of oxygen tents – an open type for young children when the expired air escapes, and the closed type where the expired air passes through a carbon dioxide absorber, and the air is cooled by passing it over ice. Mary Royles has described the setting up of the closed type used for adults. Some patients found it oppressive in the tent, with feeding and nursing more difficult to carry out.

Fire precautions were in place when oxygen was used as it is inflammable and anything likely to cause fire or sparks is avoided. No oil or grease is used on the oxygen regulator or nozzle of the cylinder. Once the tent is flooded with oxygen, the flow is adjusted to 4-5 litres per minute, providing 40-50% oxygen in the tent.

Oxygen is passed into the tent by means of an injector. The pressure of flow of oxygen causes the tent air to be siphoned out and drawn, with the oxygen, through the soda lime tank and ice-chamber to purify and cool the tent. A thermometer outside the tent is attached to the ice-chamber with the bulb inside the tent recording the temperature which is maintained at 60-65°F.

It is advisable to analyse the tent air to ensure oxygen saturation is maintained but this does not seem to have been regularly carried out.

Winnie Wilson SRN
Student Nurse, Staff Nurse, Sister [1959-1981]

Winnie Wilson was in the third group of students taking her SRN who went to Llangwyfan Hospital from Llandudno Hospital as part of her training for 3 months. She had heard a talk by Miss Morris the Matron, about Llangwyfan which sparked her interest and as her father's family came from the area it was an opportunity to get to know some of them. Her mother did not want her to do so in case she developed Tuberculosis, but she was determined and started in October 1959. She enjoyed working at Llangwyfan and said that the teaching she had received from the Nurse Tutor, Miss Kate Williams, was very good. This was during her second year as a Nurse in Llandudno General Hospital.

After she completed her training and gained the SRN she applied for a post of Staff Nurse in Llangwyfan and returned on the 1st April 1962 to be a Staff Nurse and to take part as a student on the BTA course for a year. She failed the BTA exam and did not bother to re-sit it as by then she had become a Staff Nurse in the Operating Theatre in 1963.

She enjoyed working with Mr Hugh Reid who she said was a perfect gentleman and in those days did mainly general surgery. Mr Ivor Lewis and Mr Howell Hughes did the chest work – Lobectomies and Pneumonectomies. Mr Richard Doyle did mainly Genitourinary work – many Cystoscopies, Prostatectomies and Nephrectomies. He would drive to the "Sani" on his motorised bike with his bowler hat strapped on to his case on the back of his bike. His lists were due to start at 4:00 pm on Monday, but he might not appear until 10:00 pm if he was held up in Liverpool and Winnie would not get home until 4:00 am the following morning. Monday morning was for Mr Kellett Jones to do extraction of teeth; then Miss Catrin Williams would do an occasional ENT list. Tuesday afternoon Mr Howell Hughes would do a list. Mr Lewis operated on Thursdays. There were 2-3 operating instrument sets and theatre had its own autoclave so normally lists moved smoothly.

In 1964 she was appointed a Ward Sister on Block 3, female medical mostly chest complaints. In 1965 gynaecology patients were admitted from St Asaph; mostly Mr Stewart Hunter's convalescent patients. The highlight of that era was that she and Peter had their first child, Julie, born on a Sunday afternoon in 1966, with the help of Margaret Lloyd, Sister on Block 8; the baby being put in a "drawer" and mum and baby later transferred to HM Stanley Hospital, St Asaph. A year later (1967) Ian was born and in 1970, Helen.

Winnie left her position in Llangwyfan in 1966 and returned to part-time duty in August 1968, becoming full time in 1972. Part-time nursing staff were not allowed to be Sisters and she was in the Operating Theatre covering emergencies and sharing theatre responsibilities with Sister Rosemary Holmes. When she returned to full time work, she regained her Sister position. All other theatre staff were part-time.

When patients were admitted from The Royal Alexandra Hospital, Rhyl; when that Operating Theatre was closed in the late 1960's, Sister Judith Rogers was in charge of them on Ward 8. She was the daughter of Mrs Dickens a telephonist at Llangwyfan.

Winnie stayed at Llangwyfan until it closed to patients and then moved to Abergele Hospital. She told me that it was "tough going" when she first returned to work when her youngest daughter was two years old, but between them she and Peter managed "to juggle" home and work.

Winnie has also contributed a great deal to Llandyrnog community life and is particularly interested in supporting the young.

Llangwyfan Hospital 1967/1968 – Memories by Avril Pratt (née Hughes)
Administration Sister

I only spent three months at Llangwyfan Hospital as an Administrative Sister, before returning to HM Stanley Hospital, thus not a long experience, but I hope I can give some insight into how nursing administration, particularly the role of Matron in a Sanatorium, was in those years.

Nursing was then hierarchical, Matron being the leader of her profession. This was definitely displayed by Matron Blodwen Morris – she was known by all staff – not just the Nurses, but also by patients!! In addition she was the Principal of the Hospital and her experience was acknowledged and valued by all who worked in, or visited, the Hospital. My abiding memory is our lunch time!

The staff dining room was large, with long windows facing an inside corridor. Nearly all staff ate here, except Matron and her Administrative Nursing Staff. Matron would command us all to be ready for lunch, and in order of precedence, follow her along the corridor past the staff dining room – Blod (as we called her) plus dog, Miss Allerton (Assistant Matron), Mrs Wilson, Mrs Anderson and Mrs Hughes (Administration Sisters). There was much grinning and smirking from the staff in the dining room as we marched past continuing to Matron's dining room. Here we would all be seated around the table, with Matron either carving the meat or plating our meals which were then served to each of us by the dining room maid. We sat demurely until Matron commenced her meal, when we followed suit.

Chat was low-key, but quite frequently we would find ourselves on the alert, when Blod would have a ferocious bout of choking and coughing – I soon learnt that nobody took any notice of this – as Matron having gone red in the face and looking ready to expire would soon recover, tuck her napkin under her chin and continue to eat.

On a daily basis, Matron would take tea and cakes at about 3:30 pm in her office, beautifully laid out with a china tea service. Any Hospital visitor of significance, ie Hospital Chaplain, visiting Clergy, Health Authority Personnel, local Councillors were invited and sometimes the Administrative Sister on duty was also invited to attend. As a young Administrative Sister, I was not always overjoyed to be invited to these occasions, as I really wished to be with the patients!!

For the three months at Llangwyfan, I was not really given a particular role as Administrative Sister, other than running errands or helping out the other Administrative Sisters or Assistant Matron. However, Miss Morris always kept abreast of the times, and the Salmon Report on Nursing grades had just come out, with a new role of Nursing Officer to support the Ward Sister. Matron knew I enjoyed working within the ward area, and decided I should take on this new role alongside one of the Ward Sisters.

Fortunately, the Ward Sister and I had a good working relationship, and between us we designed a role which would not step on that of the Ward Sister, but gave credence to the role of Nursing Officer. Thus on Ward 8 and 9 the embryo of Nursing Officer was created at Llangwyfan Hospital.

In my brief three months working at Llangwyfan, I remember a happy, caring community, whose staff worked with pride for the Hospital and also for their Matron.

Morfydd Hood
Sister on Hut B
[1960-1962]
with
Sally Jones, née Hughes
Staff Nurse, then Sister [1959-1981]
Staff Nurse on Hut B [1960-1962]

Sally Jones had trained as a Nurse in Liverpool gaining her SRN and decided to get her BTA in Llangwyfan. She started on Block 4 with Sister Myfanwy Jones and Sister Muriel Phillips and Dr Mayer was in charge of the block, with Dr Munro as Houseman. Dr Munro was from Inverness and married Tony Roche and they then moved to live in Australia. She was very good with patients who felt they could relate to her. Patients were graded once a week by Dr Mayer in Betty's Corner and patients were apprehensive before this was carried out in case they went backwards not forwards.

She thought that Blocks 4 and 6 changed places in 1961 as she was married in 1960 and Block 4 at that time was on the left below Block 7 and above Block 3. On her marriage, Greta Jones became her mother-in-law and Tecwyn Jones her brother-in-law. Both these are mentioned elsewhere. Tecwyn worked on nights but because Mr Doyle worked late he helped him with his genitourinary patients. Block 4 treated female patients with Pulmonary Tuberculosis. Sally had thought of becoming a Health Visitor, but after the birth of her daughter decided to go back to Llangwyfan on night duty. She eventually worked on all the wards.

Hut B, the top hut, was for male patients with various lung diseases such as Carcinoma, Bronchiectasis, Farmers Lung, etc but no Tuberculosis. If Tuberculosis was diagnosed in any patient, he was transferred to another ward. Sister Hood was in charge of Hut B and Charge Nurse Roger Jones. Charge Nurse Glyn Jones was in Hut A. Hut B was under the medical care of Dr Gallagher with Dr Hussain as the Houseman. A cousin of Sister Hood was a Chef, David Owen, who died recently and Dr Glyn Penrhyn Jones was a cousin of her father.

Many of the patients from Hut B went to Clatterbridge for Radiotherapy and then returned to Hut B. Consequently, Sister Hood decided to go to the Royal Marsden Hospital in London to extend her knowledge and was there for five years before moving to Charing Cross Hospital to open a new Radiotherapy Department. She then moved to Worcester to work in the administrative side of nursing and got married whilst she was there. In the Marsden it was known that she had worked with Ivor Lewis and she was once asked to go to the Theatre to tell the Surgeon what Mr Lewis had done for drainage of the chest. She described under water drainage, and watching the water oscillating with breathing and then how patients were sat up to cough following pneumonectomy or lobectomy. She also remembers the Brompton Cocktail being used for severe pain and this contained gin and morphia.

Llangwyfan was always kept spotlessly clean. All the beds were moved and cleaned underneath daily, damp dusting was carried out daily. Bloods were taken daily before 9 am and sent to St Asaph, and the ward was ready for the Doctors' round by 9 am. They were taught never to use their hands on the taps but to use their elbows. There was no infection like MRSA. The Huts were cold because the windows were always open, but red blankets were put on the bottom of all beds in case the patient was cold. Also there was a Macintosh cover to go over it as well as over trolleys if the patient needed to go to X-ray. The nursing staff were provided with umbrellas to cover them and the patient if the weather was inclement.

Patients did well after surgery and on all wards the Tuberculosis regime was carried out; rest, fresh air and physiotherapy. It was a very busy hospital, a good hospital and results were brilliant, and they agreed that they had learnt a lot there. Hugh Reid was a perfect gentleman and would come in the evening to see his patients as he lived locally. Ivor Lewis was "on his own" – Sally spoke Welsh with him, Morfydd English.

On one occasion a Surgeon from Rhyl came to do a Tracheotomy, the first time Sally saw this being done. She remembers Miss Catrin Williams doing proof puncture of the antra and leaving fine plastic tubes in place so that washouts could be carried out until the antra were clear. Night Staff would do this with saline night and morning, then Day Staff during the day.

When Miss Morris, Matron, did a ward round her corgi called Jane would accompany her. They liked Miss Coombs the Deputy Matron also and said she was lovely.

Opposite Hut B was a Hut where the dishes from Tuberculosis patients were washed and dried. Hut A was the next hut down and opposite was the hut with the Pulmonary Function Room, Plaster Room and Occupational Therapy Room – with Miss Rich in charge. Below Hut A was Hut D and opposite Hut C. Huts A, D and C were for Tuberculosis patients. In the 1960's Nurses were living in the bottom huts and Sisters in Cwyfan. Sally Jones and three other staff Nurses shared bedrooms in Jack Harnell's big house in Denbigh. They rented their accommodation and made their own food.

Children would be taken for walks every day and there were also trips by coach. The grounds were beautifully kept and the pond. It was a friendly place to nurse, where everyone knew each other and there was no back-biting, but a nice atmosphere and it was safe to walk between blocks on night duty. If Sally Jones walked from Block 7 to Block 9, a Nurse would watch her and she would wave when she arrived. They sometimes had to take patients to the Mortuary with an Orderly to help and they would visit the Boiler Houseman 2 to 3 times a night to make sure he was alright.

CHAPTER 9.2

MEMORIES OF GENERAL STAFF

Jean McLellan MSR
[Radiographer, 1962-1975]

I enjoyed my visit to see Jean McLellan and her sister Margaret in Llanrhaeadr. She had been a Radiographer at Llangwyfan from 1962-1975. At this time Dr Biagi was in charge with Dr Gallagher as his Deputy. She had heard that Dr Gallagher had become unwell and returned to Ireland after she retired. I was sorry as this story confirmed what I had heard earlier. Dr Gallagher had been a very nice lady and good Doctor, especially with children. Jean remembered Dr Bapat and of his research into Farmers Lung. Miss Morris was the Matron, and was friendly with Staff Nurse Tinseley of the Children's Ward. Because of this people were very careful with and what they said in front of Staff Nurse Tinseley and were wary of her.

Unfortunately, Jean has no photographs of her time in Llangwyfan, nor of the X-ray Department. She remembers Block 9 Staff, as this was next to X-ray and of Sister Freda Jones who moved to Block 3 and is now dead. Jean followed Tony Roache as a Radiographer. His wife was a Doctor, Dr Alison Munro, and they went to Australia after 3 years. Margaret Coop who married Kellett Jones, the Dental Surgeon, would occasionally cover Jean's work when she went away on holiday. Margaret was a Radiographer in the early 1950's.

Jean was kept busy all day, at first taking 15-30 X-rays mainly chest work. When this declined she X-rayed postoperative patients from Rhyl, patients with Bronchitis, Coronaries, Farmer's Lung and Orthopaedic problems. She does not remember Mr Stewart Hunter but could get called for convalescing gynaecology patients transferred from St Asaph. She normally worked from 9am-5pm but could get called at any time and when Dickie Doyle did his lists he was often late arriving and it could be late when she got home, but no-one minded the long hours or disruption caused. All staff were X-rayed once a year and she X-rayed the night staff when Mr Doyle did his lists.

Gwyn Griffiths was the X-ray Porter and I have fond memories of him helping in the Operating Theatre, and Menna Ellis was the Darkroom Technician. She said that she was kept busy all day in the early days but the last 3-4 years were very quiet and she was deployed at times in Denbigh, St Asaph and Rhyl X-ray Departments.

Dr Rodney Green, the Senior Radiologist, she knew in Liverpool in Broadgreen Hospital. He got Pulmonary Tuberculosis from a patient in Aintree Hospital and she X-rayed him many times. When she appeared in Llangwyfan he said "oh it's you". He had been a patient in Aintree for a year. Dr Gordon Row was not in Liverpool when she was there. Dr Biagi did not throw anything away and when they had a very famous actor as a patient, she decided later to find his X-rays and did so. She had been trained in Southport Hospital, being a student in the X-ray Department for 2 years and went to Liverpool Royal Infirmary for lectures, and became a member of the State Register of Radiographers (MSR).

She stayed in Southport for a further 3 years after qualifying and then worked in Aintree and Fazakerley Hospitals – the former was a Tuberculosis Hospital and the latter for Infectious Diseases, from 1953-1962. She then obtained the post in Llangwyfan from 1962-1975, retiring on grounds of ill health.

During this time she lived with her sister Margaret and her mother in Penllwyn, which was a long bungalow amalgamated from 3 cottages, higher up the hillside than Vron Yw. This was owned by the Hospital and had a brick bread oven, and the date 1593 on one wall. As her mother lived with them she would go home for lunch.

Below Penllwyn was another cottage Islwyn, occupied by an Under-Gardener, Tom Evans, who had one son who became an Orderly and twin daughters who trained as nurses in Clatterbridge Hospital. Mrs Tom Evans also became an Orderly. Below Islwyn was Erw Vron occupied by Miss Behrens who was rather gruff and difficult to get to know. She kept dogs and would take them out for walks with a hunting horn to call them back. When they moved to Penllwyn they were given a choice of wallpaper and chose a pretty one for the hall, but when they got there they found that it had been papered a hideous pink colour with fish on it. She complained and was told that it was a mistake and the paper was changed.

Dr Cameron, who had lived earlier in Penllwyn and in 1962 was in a wheelchair, called to ask if he could see the house again. She liked all the people she worked with and work conditions were good. She told me that Mr Howell Hughes carried out a procedure on her and I gave her the anaesthetic to which she had an allergic reaction, and I warned her not to have this particular drug again. She told me that she was allergic to so many things and had reactions to them – but following my warning she had 2 further operations without ill-effect, but remembered consequently that she had had a general anaesthetic aged 19 years and been asked afterwards how long she'd had a bad chest, and wondered whether she'd had an allergic reaction then but had not been told about it. She said Mr Ivor Lewis was "lovely, really" and understood she couldn't learn Welsh.

When Psychogeriatric patients came they were X-rayed once a year. They were housed in the huts higher up than Ward 9. She agreed with Dr Amir (Anaesthetist) that the theatre light was static and the table had to be moved to get the operating field under the light. She retired in 1975 and has had to use a wheelchair since 1989, at first being able to walk around her home, but for the last year she has been unable to do this. She has never been depressed and has an indomitable courage in facing her disability.

Another Dark Room Technician she had from 1965-1967 was Mari Evans whose father had been farm Bailiff to Lady Graham. Mari had helped me to look after my children before taking up this post. She told me that the Physiotherapist before Graham Day was Norman Brookes. He had worked in Ruthin Castle when it was a Nursing Home and when this closed in 1962 he had moved to Llangwyfan where he stayed until 1968/69, when he left to take up a post in the North Wales Hospital, Denbigh. Mr Day was there for about 5 years and committed suicide, which was a terrible shock for everyone as no-one had any inkling that he had had any problems.

Joan Gwenllian Hughes

Joan Gwenllian Hughes was offered the post of Senior Occupational Therapist in January 1961 and stayed for approximately two years. She remembers having the pleasure of riding pillion to work on Miss Wolstencroft's motor cycle which she recalled as a most enjoyable experience. She also points out the difference in salary scales between those days and today. The Occupational Therapy Department was in one of the huts, but she has not been able to contact Miss Rose Wolstencroft or Miss Margaret Rich but has sent me photographs of those days.

Paul Williams,
Porter [1978-1979 for 4 months]

Paul was born in Bristol, lived in Cardiff at first, then his parents moved to Denbigh where he grew up. He started work as a Relief Porter on the 2nd October 1978, shadowing Goronwy Morris and Willie Plumb, who left at the end of October to go to Glan Clwyd as Security Staff and part of the Commissioning Staff. So he learnt from them what to do and his way around the scattered buildings.

His work entailed walking a lot, moving patients around blocks and delivering laundry, meals and stores to the blocks. There was a lot of lifting to do and he learnt to be methodical in order to make deliveries smoother at the blocks, for some blocks had more deliveries than others. To assist, they drove electric or battery powered trolleys – one being a van and two were open – and he loaded the packs on to these. Everything was labelled, but he didn't open them.

There were two shifts:- 7:30 am to 4:30 pm (early) or 12:30 mid-day to 9:00 pm (late shift). Work was busy but not exhausting, a nice atmosphere without hassle or aggravation. He said that what was important was the fact that there was a Matron (Charge Nurse Lloyd) who knew the hospital and knew what was required.

There were unpleasant duties, such as the collection, counting and disposal of the contents of the stainless steel spittoons, which were collected in the morning, taken to the area where there was a steam boiler, and thrown into it. Sometimes they would get an urgent call from a ward that a patient had lost their dentures mistakenly, having deposited them in the wrong container the previous evening (not in the denture mug). Then it was panic to try and save them before they melted in the heat. They did not measure the amount of sputum in the spittoons; this had already been carried out on the Ward.

Another unpleasant task was to take bodies to the Mortuary and take a rough measurement of the body for the Undertaker. If a body had been taken across at night they had to measure it in the morning, making sure that all documents were in order, and making a note of what jewellery was on the body and fill in a Record Book with the correct details.

They had to make sure that the Operating Theatre had an ample supply of gases in cylinders. These were stored in a room near the X-ray Department and secured by lock and key. This room had a louvered door.

The day had a pattern, starting with taking breakfast to the blocks. Each ground floor block had its own trolley and the upstairs wards had food delivered in boxes, delivered by the truck and carried upstairs. Meals were not set out as happens now but portions were divided by the Ward Staff which he thought was a better idea as the senior staff knew the patients and how much they could eat and made sure they ate it, so there was less waste. Then they sorted out the delivery of laundry, supplies, post and case notes from office to wards.

They took a mid-morning break when work permitted and lunch was between 12:00 mid-day and 1:00 pm. He took his own food but he knew the hospital food couldn't be faulted, and this was taken after the patients had theirs.

In the afternoon patients might be taken to X-ray or admissions might be taken to the wards after they had been dropped off at the main block and the ambulance had to leave. They would then be taken to the ward by truck.

When he started there were 6 Porters in all, with Gordon Holmes as Head Porter – including Trevor Lloyd, Charlie Hughes, Albert Owen and Gary. After Goronwy Morris and Willie Plumb left a temporary Porter called Chris was taken on so they were down to 5. As long as he thought what he needed to do and planned the day, work was not an issue.

They knew Glan Clwyd was going to be opened and

Llangwyfan would be shut and in the middle of December 1978 an advert appeared for staff interested in moving to Glan Clwyd as they were looking for staff to accept deliveries of supplies to the hospital. They were also looking for Porters to move items from stores to various departments. He applied and was accepted starting in Glan Clwyd on 15 January 1979.

When Glan Clwyd opened in May 1980 everyone knew everyone in the hospital and it was a very friendly place, unlike today when there was a lot of pressure, people didn't know each other. "it is unbelievable how things have gone".

Of the characters in Llangwyfan he remembers Emlyn Bach who did odd jobs in the Boiler House and gardens. He had a push bike covered with flags and pennants and also had a trailer behind it at times. He lived in Llandyrnog and would wave at everyone and was very funny.

One of Paul's other tasks was to carry a lot of old books and papers from the Administration Block to the incinerator in the Boiler House. These were all boxed up ready for him to take. "such a lot of stuff went". A lot of stuff was brought from Colwyn Bay Hospital, the Royal Alexandra and War Memorial Hospitals in Rhyl and taken to the old huts near the Chapel. These were two old Army Huts.

He doesn't remember seeing iron lungs, although a lot of material was boxed in storage. He was most friendly with maintenance staff and gardeners as these were the people he saw daily. Everyone worked well together and were prepared to do odd jobs like handymen. Now there is Health and Safety precluding this.

In January 1979 Porters had left to go to Glan Clwyd. One left to join the Royal Mail, one left to join security in Glan Clwyd and one was left on his own in Llangwyfan.

Paul went to see Gwyn Evans, the Theatre Superintendent in Glan Clwyd to see if there were vacancies to be trained in the Theatre, but the only vacancy at that time was in the Theatre

Services Centre (TSC). He applied, was interviewed and accepted; being the only male with 7 or 8 females and remained there 8-9 months. TSC was run by Sister Pat Ellis and they sterilized all the instruments used in Theatre. Packs still continued to be sent to CSSD in HM Stanley Hospital which was run by Mrs Gwen Bird. He stayed 6½ years and was then accepted for training as a Technician.

He is now the Lead Operating Department Practitioner in the Eye Theatre at HM Stanley Hospital and has been there 10 years. He loves the work; every day being different and it is never boring.

The move to Glan Clwyd was a sad time. The change from Sanatorium to a Convalescent or Mini Hospital necessitated a change and they knew the new hospital was coming, but it was a pity that no role could be found for Llangwyfan. About a year ago he walked past it up the lane to Vron Yw and was saddened by what he saw. I have also walked there and seen the dereliction of the huts at both sites, but the main buildings which cannot be seen have had a re-vamp and are of quality. Many buildings have gone that were used for storage and the Power House has gone as well.

He said that the gardens made Llangwyfan a special place with open grounds, lawns which were well maintained and a pond below Blocks 8 and 9 at the bottom of the slope. The latter has been removed but the grounds still remain well maintained. Trees and shrubs have grown and it is a more secretive place now than it was when the cover of Llangwyfan Sanatorium to Hospital was photographed in the 1920's.

Memories – Helen Roberts

Helen Roberts started working in Llangwyfan in 1961 becoming a Secretary in the main office and undertaking general duties. Helen's father was Emrys Roberts and appears in a Porters photograph next to Gwyn Griffiths. When patients arrived by ambulance she would go into the ambulance to take their details and when these had been completed the ambulance would take the patient to the ward. In 1978 she left to become part of the Commissioning Team in Glan Clwyd. There were not many staff there then and they did not have much to do but she remained as a member of the administration staff when the hospital opened and would often play the organ in the YGC Chapel Services. In Llangwyfan she often baby-sat for Dr Penrhyn Jones' children.

She admired Miss Salt, Hospital Secretary, who looked after staff well in Llangwyfan, and felt that she was strong and fair. When she was in a bad mood she would hum and play with her bunch of keys. William Roberts, the Group Chief Executive, didn't often go to Llangwyfan but would attend House Committees where there were eight to ten members, including Mrs Haf Lewis Jones, whose husband was a General Practitioner in Ruthin.

She remembers four bottom huts; 1, 2, 3 and 4 and two garages for hospital transport, one for a car and one for a bus. Hospital records were kept in the top hut and these continued to be housed there for some time. Matron Morris was a very good organiser and there was a good social life with cheese and wine parties, fancy dress and an annual dance.

Memories – Jean Moffat

I have a lot of links to Llangwyfan Hospital, my mother worked there for many years, my stepfather also worked there and in fact he was found dead on duty in the Power House in 1970. I was a patient there from 1955 to 1957, then again in 1958 to 1959. I knew Staff Nurse Tinseley when I was a patient on Ward 8. As children we were all very frightened of her, she seemed to have more authority than the Sister of the ward, in fact I recall that a majority of the staff were in awe of her, I don't know why!! Dr Gallagher was the children's doctor, she was a lovely lady all the children including me loved her. Dr Biagi was the Consultant of the hospital, he was a very clever man and much admired and respected by both patients and staff, I lived in 4 Fron Yw Cottages. When I left school I worked as a dining room attendant and later on I worked as a Nursing Auxiliary and I knew Matron Morris when I was a patient and she employed me for both my posts. She was a typical Matron of her day, she did an excellent job and was respected by everyone. Both my children were christened in Llangwyfan Church and my late son, stepfather and my Mother are buried there.

Mossie Royles, Chef
[1952-1964]

Mossie was trained as a Chef in the Army at the Army Catering Core, for two years in the Aldershot School of Catering. When he left the Army he was living in Tremeirchion and the only job advert he found locally in the Employment Exchange was at Llangwyfan. He applied and was interviewed for the post by Miss Morrison, the Matron, who was very strict; and was successful.

He thought the kitchen in Llangwyfan was old fashioned and

the stove needed stoking with anthracite and the fish fryer with coal and coke which made them unpredictable, and they depended on the weather. Later an electric stove which was more reliable was purchased.

He worked different shifts on a rota. The early one was 6:00am to 2:00 pm, the next 8:00am to 5:00pm and the late 12:00 midnight to 8:00 am. Although staff were paid extra if they worked late, he preferred the early shift. There were six cooks altogether, assisted by six domestics and three kitchen porters. On a shift there would be two cooks, two domestics and one porter. All staff got on well together.

Menus were drawn up for a week in advance by the Head Chef. At first this was done by Mr Carlyle; he was followed by Miss Edwards who was also ex-army and then by Miss Lyn Jones who died two years ago aged 90 years. The food was then ordered by the Catering Officer.

Cooking breakfast for 480 staff and patients took two hours. An item in the Daily Express in 1960-1961 said that Llangwyfan had the best food in a hospital in the country and was highly recommended. It included a discussion on feeding patients. Everyone I spoke to during interviewing told me what wonderful food Llangwyfan produced and he was pleased to hear that.

Mid-day dinner took three hours to prepare with Porters cleaning potatoes and Domestics cleaning and washing the pots. The staff would have their dinner after serving the others in the Dining Room.

Teatime was only a cup of tea and cake, and supper was a meal like lunch, which was cooked. There was a little choice but they catered for patients on special diets and diabetics, etc.

The work was busy but the staff were friendly and they had "a good laugh". They catered for parties and the Christmas Panto-mimes and Christmas as described elsewhere was a special time.

MEMORIES OF PATIENTS

Aida Groome [1920-2007]
Testimony by her husband, Ted

Aida was a patient in Llangwyfan from March 1953 - May 1954.
Ted and Aida were married in Clwyd Street Chapel, Rhyl in
July 1945. Ted was in the Army and was posted to Rangoon. On
the way there the Atom Bomb was dropped, bringing World War
II to an end and his ship was diverted to Naples, and half the
unit was sent to Italy. Six months later Aida joined him in Naples
and they had a holiday in Amalfi. After a fortnight his unit was
moved to Northern Italy, there were no married quarters but
they found accommodation. Aida developed Pleurisy and was
admitted to Padua Military Hospital followed by 2 weeks
convalescence in Austria. They moved to Venice, then Vicensa, for
a year followed by 2 years in Tripoli. It was a very unsettled life
but they were always positive and went where they were
required.

When she became pregnant she went home to her parents in
Rhyl to Grove Park and would walk to see her GP in the surgery
in Bath Street, Dr McQueen or Dr Anderson. She gave birth to a
son, John, on 28th February 1953. Ted was at that time with the
forces in the Canal Zone but got home for the birth which was
delayed 3 weeks and he had to return shortly after Aida and
John came home, but there was just time to have him christened
in Clwyd Street Chapel.

Shortly after his return he heard that Aida had Pleurisy and was back in Hospital in St Asaph, leaving John to be cared for by her parents. Within days she was transferred to Llangwyfan where she remained for 14 months. Although it was a terrible blow they were fortunate that John's Grandparents came to their rescue. Aida's brother helpfully arranged through SSAFA for Ted to be recalled to the UK for 6 months compassionate leave and he was attached to Headquarters, Midwest District at Shrewsbury allowing him to travel to Rhyl every weekend.

Aida, through contacts in the Hospital, employed a nursemaid from Ruthin called Mair, to look after John in her parent's home and this arrangement lasted over a year; Mair living with the family. Ted would return to Rhyl every weekend by train on Friday evening from Shrewsbury. On Saturday he went to Denbigh and would go to Aida's Auntie's home to borrow a bike to cycle to Llangwyfan having lunch in a pub in Llandyrnog on the way. He would walk up to the Hospital to spend the afternoon with Aida until 5:00 pm. On Sunday he would borrow a relative's car to drive John and his grandparents to Llangwyfan so that Aida saw her baby son once a week at the gates. On Sunday evening he would take the train back to Shrewsbury. Aida gradually became strong enough to have a one stage Thoracoplasty by Mr Ivor Lewis.

Although I knew Aida, I did not know her medical history until after her death so was unable to question her of her feelings at being deprived of her baby. I can only imagine how difficult it had been. It shows she was resourceful in getting help to look after her baby and how fortunate she was that the war was over and Ted could be stationed in this country for six months. She was a charming, friendly lady with a good sense of humour and I always felt she had a philosophical outlook on life. Her experience in Llangwyfan had perhaps influenced this.

She was born in Chubut, Patagonia to Welsh speaking and Welsh born parents. Her father, John Jones, was born in Dyserth some four miles from Rhyl and he and his brothers became Builders. Peter Morris Jones (PM) and W T Jones were well known in Rhyl and built many bungalows in the town. John decided to go to the United States of America and went to Liverpool to get a passport, but through talking to someone in the queue changed his mind and decided to go instead to Argentina in 1910. Her mother was born in Llanrwst and because her brother wanted to go to Patagonia she decided to go with him and take her sewing machine, attaining a job as a Dressmaker. It was there that she met and married John Jones (JJ). They had three children; Aida being the youngest born in 1920. JJ, her father, became a Builder of Chapels in the Chubut Valley and later when Aida was six years he moved to Buenos Aires where he became the Master Builder of the Railway Station. After six months, when he had established himself, he sent for his family from Chubut. The children spoke Welsh and Spanish and all were Argentinian citizens and had Argentinian passports.

In 1934 they returned to Wales and at the outbreak of World War II, as they had Argentinian passports, the children were regarded as aliens, put into quarantine and had to report to the Police Station every week. She had to have permission from the Police to ride a bike and was not allowed to do factory work or join the Armed Services. She got a job in a Grocery Shop in Denbigh and stayed with an aunt whose husband was the Station Master of Denbigh. Later, she became a Land Girl and was trained in Llysfasi College before working on a farm in Caerwys. She also volunteered to help in the YMCA on a Sunday, serving breakfast and there met her future husband who was coming to the end of his training as an apprentice in the Royal Artillery, repairing engineering equipment used by Gunners.

Memories: Dewi Roberts

When I was in my twenties I was unfortunate enough to develop a duodenal ulcer. My GP felt that surgery would probably be inevitable and I was referred to Mr Jonathan's Clinic. As a result my name was added to a surgical list. Eventually a letter arrived asking me to report to the Alexandra Hospital, where I would be admitted to await surgery – or so I thought! I sat around in the ward on arrival and shortly after lunch the Sister came to tell me that I would not be admitted after all, but would be transferred to Llangwyfan.

I was delighted when I arrived there, to discover myself accommodated in a cubicle rather than an open ward, for I have always valued my privacy. I do not recall which block I was in but do remember the very friendly atmosphere. My treatment was purely a dietary one; lots of boiled fish, rice pudding and other foods which many might well consider bland. I ate what was put in front of me gladly in the hope that it would heal the ulcer. I was fortunate enough to be at Llangwyfan during a lovely summer – I think it may have been 1963 – and was permitted to get dressed each day and given the freedom to walk in the grounds. Unknown to the staff, I made the ascent to Offa's Dyke one day. I also did a lot of reading and would engage in literary discussion with a dietician who came around frequently. I recall exchanging views on "Catch 22" with her. I treated my three week stay at Llangwyfan as a kind of holiday, although it was made quite clear that the village pub at Llandyrnog was out of bounds!

Dr Biagi was in charge of the hospital then and he was extremely keen to stamp out smoking on the part of patients. It was said that he would walk around the hospital looking for evidence, usually in the form of cigarette stubs. Possibly my abiding memory of that spell in Llangwyfan was the magnificent view which one could obtain over the vale of Clwyd.

Medically, all the boiled fish worked and I have never experienced similar problems since.

Memories: Laura Mullen (d. 2008)

Laura Mullen was another patient who was admitted to Llangwyfan for surgery in 1974 under the care of Mr Jonathan. She was in Block 9 for a fortnight which was longer than usual due to developing a complication, later moving to another block and being there in total for three weeks. She found the staff excellent, an integration of Rhyl and Llangwyfan staff who mixed well together. She remembered having a bed bath from a very nice Scottish Sister from the Theatre which was bliss. She remembered it was a warm place in February, where she was happy with the care she had received as well as the food. Medical staff from Rhyl including Mr Jonathan visited often.

Memories: Douglas Vernon (d. 1st April 2007)

He was a patient in Llangwyfan for 3 months in 1972 suffering from a heart condition, a patient of Dr Biagi. Douglas was a keen gardener and enjoyed sitting in his wheelchair in the grounds of Llangwyfan. He was allowed home at weekends and the Llangwyfan gardener would give him snippets of some of the shrubs for him to plant in his own garden. They thrived and Douglas and his wife Brenda would say that the row of small shrubs which they cultivated looked like a mini Llangwyfan.

Brenda, his wife, would visit Douglas using the Llangwyfan bus. They both found all the staff wonderfully dedicated and Douglas benefited by the treatment and remained a keen gardener winning many first prizes at the Denbigh Shows, continuing to garden even after he suffered a stroke. He won first prize for his own garden, which he tended from his electric wheelchair, enjoying it until his death.

Gwyn Pierce-Williams MB BCh(Liverpool) DRCOG, MRCGP, DFFP

Gwyn wrote:-

"In January 1962 I was a patient at Llangwyfan, where I had my eighth birthday. Remembering the journey there, the District Nurse drove me and my mother in her car from Holyhead; it seemed the longest journey I'd ever done. We went into the first building which was like a grand reception. Quite a frightening place the Administration Building. I was taken to Ward 8, the Children's Ward, with my mother and then she was admitted to Ward 4.

When I saw there were other children I settled down a bit. There were roughly 15-16 boys and girls there at a time, with the sexes segregated, girls to the left and boys to the right. A weekly bath and hair wash took place on Saturday night before Sunday visiting. It was strange to put the children in Ward 8 close to the Theatre Block – Block 9, because of the noise from the children, although no-one from Block 9 complained. The Auxiliary Nurses were best with kids. [In the Theatre we didn't hear the children – BO].

The Ward had double doors, which we weren't allowed through, but I was taken through them once to see my mother in Block 9, after she had her operation she was a patient in Block 4, down the hill. Then a second time to get my teeth taken out under a general anaesthetic. I had to drink a foul green liquid beforehand, then I remember the fight, as this hard mask was pressed against my face, hitting out at the Anaesthetist.

I used to pass by my mother's Ward sometimes and see her at the window.

There were the kindly staff and the very strict staff. There were people who helped at mealtimes – the first meal there was rissoles. I've hated the bloody things every since. There was a lovely Auxiliary Nurse called Blod, who used to secrete my black pudding so I didn't have to eat it. The table was in front of the window and I passed the black puddings once to an Orderly outside.

The first winter there was a lot of snow and we had great fun playing on the slopes outside the Wards. We slid down on trays from the kitchen. We used to climb the trees at the back and bring frogs and wood pigeon eggs into our lockers by each bed as personal trophies. We got into trouble when we got found out. We also killed cockroaches at night in the kitchen of our block by hitting them with dressing gown cord, but the Night Nurses paid no attention.

School was most afternoons. We did general stuff – English, Maths, Kitchen Science, Nature. Kitchen Science was science applied to household materials. This was undertaking simple experiments with Starch, Iodine, detergents etc using what was available. There were also simple nature lessons to do with plants. These were exciting and it broke up the monotony of the day. We had a cub pack as well – once a week after tea. Funny thing about that was that they only had bits of uniform which had to be shared out – some people had a hat, some a jumper, some a tie – at the beginning of the night you dipped into the box to see what you could get. We were a right motley crew! There were no formal organised games but we played around a lot. We also did handiwork such as crochet and used reeds to make baskets – I didn't keep any of it.

All the treatments were done in the morning. Medication was a horrible powder stuff, then I had a course of injections following an episode of haemoptysis. The reason for this was that we had been playing with a sucker type bow and arrow in the corridor, we shot it then we rushed to get the arrow – whoever got it first got the next go. I stumbled and the arrow went down my throat. I coughed up blood and I was sentenced to an additional six weeks of injections for TB! There were weekly ward rounds from Dr Gallagher, quite relaxed affairs, but it was a strict and severe affair when Dr Biagi came around. There was a hairdresser – a man who came around once in a while and cut everyone's hair with an actual pudding bowl and electric clippers.

The real treat was of course the cinema. Once a month a huge screen was brought in to the Ward by the Porters, an old projector set up, and we were all given a box of chocolates as we sat down to watch the film! I didn't understand much English at the time so I didn't understand the films, but I understood that the chocolates were coming!

There were some Welsh speaking children there and we stuck together – there was one boy, Peter, with whom I was always fighting. He spoke English, and that was probably part of the problem.

The highlight of life, however, was the frequent weekends when my mother would hire the cottage in the grounds, by the pond, for the day or for the weekend. Visitors would visit you there; relatives could stay there overnight. There was a kitchen for preparing snacks or a cup of tea. It was much more relaxed and people could spend much longer with you, especially if travelling from Anglesey, rather than sticking to visiting hours. I remember Ann, my cousin from Menai Bridge, came for the day.

I was ready to go out long before my mother, but had to wait for her to be discharged before I could go. They had had to build her up to a certain weight before she had her operation.

In the latter part of my stay, Auntie Mag brought me a little radio, which I kept on Radio Luxembourg, and listened under the pillow – I learnt a lot of English from that and my English improved during that time.

It wasn't his Llangwyfan experience that was the deciding factor in Gwyn's decision to become a Doctor. He told me that this was made at an earlier time as he hero-worshipped their General Practitioner in Holyhead – Dr Emyr ap Cynan (Cynan's son) and was determined to follow in his footsteps. His Llangwyfan experience did not deviate him from this decision and he is a highly respected General Practitioner in Rhyl, who is now the Medical Director of Denbighshire Local Health Board.

I remember Gwyn coming to the Royal Alexandra Hospital, Rhyl in 1977 as Houseman to Mr Owen Daniel. He married Eileen, a Scottish lass, who learnt some Welsh and who was appointed to my post as Consultant Anaesthetist in Ysbyty Glan Clwyd in 1991 when I retired.

Gwyn and Eileen had 2 children – Owain, who teaches music and Arwel a Management Trainee in the NHS.

I asked Gwyn what he had learnt in Llangwyfan. The first was English and the second, self-sufficiency. As an only child, it had been a very hard time for him as his father had died seven months previously. As they lived in a tied house they had to leave their home and moved 7 times in the first year, eventually living in Llangefni. He was separated from this mother when he got to Llangwyfan and therefore had to learn how to stand on his own feet. His memory depicts a fun-loving little boy who was frightened at first but learnt to adapt in an alien environment.

Elizabeth Edwards

Elizabeth Edwards was seven years old when she was admitted to Llangwyfan for surgery on her knock-knees. She lived with her family in Vron Yw Cottages and was seen playing by Dr Biagi who told her mother she wouldn't be able to walk later in life unless this was treated. She was admitted to Ward 8 where she remembered Staff Nurse Tinseley as being very strict, Auntie Lil an Auxiliary Nurse always laughing and Little Blod, another Auxiliary. She was operated on by Mr Howell Hughes and was told that he had come especially from Liverpool. She remembered the Operating Theatre but not the anaesthetic. When she woke up she was in plaster from her toes to her chest, with a space for toileting and was nursed flat. A wooden bar was fixed across her legs to immobilise her and to be used to lift her. She remembers itching under the plaster and tried to push a knitting needle down under it to scratch the skin.

She was in hospital over Christmas, in total for six months. When the plaster was removed she had to learn to walk again, which was very painful as there had been muscle wasting. Her bed in Ward 8 overlooked the pond and Eleanor, her cousin, remembered her brother telling her that he went to a firework display near the pond and saw the reflection of the fireworks in the water. She gave me permission to publish a photograph of Margaret Joy Griffiths and a friend standing near the gardens of the bungalows where her father Iorwerth Jones was working, showing the Power House which has now been demolished.

Her father and his two brothers are shown in a photograph of 1932. They all worked in Llangwyfan – Ifor as a Farm Worker and William and Iorwerth as Gardeners; Iorwerth had previously worked on the farm and both later developed Farmers Lung. Bill Savage, the Hospital Carpenter/Joiner is shown in one photograph. He made Eleanor, Elizabeth's cousin, a wooden cradle which exemplifies his high craftsmanship. Another photograph shows Mrs Dickens, the Telephonist, who was widowed young and whom I was told was very motherly and pleasant.

In 1972 Elizabeth was admitted for a second time to Llangwyfan with Pulmonary Tuberculosis, but this time only stayed for four months. She told me that Dr Hawkins sent ten shillings every year to her father Iorwerth Jones, asking him to decorate the Hawkins window in Llangwyfan Church for Christmas.

Dr Biagi looked after her on both admissions, and she remembered Mr Howell Hughes seeing her when he visited, otherwise it was the nursing staff she remembered, especially Staff Nurse Tinseley.

CHAPTER 9.4

MEMORIES
– WIDOWS OF MEDICAL STAFF

Mair Penrhyn Jones
Widow of **Dr Glyn Penrhyn Jones [1921-1973]**

I had not kept in touch with Dr Glyn Penrhyn Jones and his family when they left Llangwyfan, but I sent Mair, his widow, a copy of "Llangwyfan, Sanatorium to Hospital" for Buddug their youngest child who had been named after me, and I got a newsy letter in return giving the history of their children and also news of Dr Novak who had appeared in a photograph; and a group photograph which included him.

Dr Novak was a Polish Doctor who had been detained in Auschwitz. After the war he came to Llangwyfan and his wife and daughter visited him and wanted him to return with them but he was afraid of the communist regime. I was told he was a very nice man and a good Doctor, and the family had been entertained for a meal with the Penrhyn Jones. Later he changed his mind and returned to Poland and they received a letter from him, from Gdansk, telling them all was well with them. He was an example of the safe haven provided by Llangwyfan to refugees.

The year 1956 had been momentous for the Penrhyn Jones family. Glyn had gained an MA in the Department of Celtic Studies, winning the O.Templeman Prize. Sion had been born and Lowri and Gruffydd started attending the Welsh Language

School in Gellifor with Morfudd Phillips (née Lloyd) as their Teacher. Quite a culture shock after living in Liverpool.

Buddug was also born when they lived in Llangwyfan. She and Lowri did a Diploma in Nursing at the Middlesex Hospital. Lowri then went to Nottingham University and did an Honours Degree in French. Buddug gained a Diploma in Health Visiting. Both are now married with three children each.

Gruffydd met his future wife, Lisa, in Atlantic College, Llantwit Major and they married before Gruffydd graduated in medicine. Lisa had been born in Finland, the family then moving to Sweden. Lisa and their children are Welsh speaking. For a time Gruffydd worked in Lapland, but is now a General Practitioner in Waenfawr, living not far from his mother.

Sion became a computer expert, married Linda and they have 2 children, Catrin who graduated in Leeds in Business Studies and Gwawr who has a degree in English from Cardiff. Catrin went to Sandhurst and then as Lieutenant Penrhyn Jones she is now in Afghanistan which is a big responsibility. Sion has travelled abroad with work and flies to Canada for one week a month on business.

It was a big loss to his family that Glyn, such a fit man, had died so young and he would be very proud of how his family has developed. I wrote about him in 'Llangwyfan Sanatorium to Hospital', where he was Deputy Medical Superintendent (1955-1959) and left to take up an appointment as Consultant Geriatrician in Ysbyty Gwynedd.

Mrs P Edwards [-1973]
Widow of **Dr Owen Edwards**

Mrs P Edwards, the widow of Dr Owen Edwards, lived with him for 2 years in Llangwyfan in the late 1950's / early 1960's. Her husband trained in Liverpool and worked in Llangwyfan for 2 years as a Registrar, following which he went to Llandudno as a Medical Registrar to Dr Makinson. Whilst there he developed a brain tumour and had surgery in Manchester Royal Infirmary and recovered. However, he was unable to continue as a Medical Registrar and changed to Public Health following advice and training by Professor Andrew Sample, Professor of Public Health in Liverpool. He was appointed Assistant Medical Officer of Health for Liverpool and Thornby moving to become Deputy Medical Officer of Health for Caernarfon for 10 years. He died in 1973.

She remembers the days in Llangwyfan as great days, of one big happy family living next door to Miss Blodwen Morris, Miss Coombs and Miss Tinseley, who lived in Orchard. She remembered Iorwerth Jones, the Gardener and Savage Jones the Carpenter – who made book shelves for her. Dr Penrhyn Jones was there for part of the time and was followed by Dr Bolser.

They had 2 daughters, Nia and Gwenan. Nia was born in HM Stanley Hospital, St Asaph. After medical training she worked in the Department of Care of the Elderly in Ysbyty Glan Clwyd before gaining a Consultant post in North Yorkshire. Gwenan became a well known Newscaster for S4C and BBC2 and is regularly seen on our television screens. She is married to Chris Low who is also a Newscaster and they live in Buckinghamshire.

Dr Novak
Medical Officer

Dr Novak was born in Poland on the 8th November 1911. He entered Warsaw Univeristy to study Medicine and qualified in March 1938. In March 1939 he joined the Polish Regular Force and worked in Warsaw Hospitals until he was interned in 1943 in Auschwitz. He was liberated in 1945 then worked in the Prisoner of War Camp under the Allies at Schwerin from May to September. In February 1946 he was working with the Polish 2nd Corps in Italy and came to England in October with his Regiment. He was held in very high regard by his superiors and wanted to work in the UK and not return to Poland. He then became a Medical Officer in Llangwyfan where he is remembered with affection.

MEMORIES – LEAGUE OF FRIENDS

Memories of
The Llangwyfan League of Hospital Friends

Mabel Lloyd Hughes was involved for 10 years as Vice-Chairman of Llangwyfan League of Friends, having been elected to this office soon after joining. The Chairman was Mrs Suzy Hughes, wife of Henry Hughes, and aunt of Dr Ceri Salusbury – a GP in Denbigh, whose mother was Suzy's sister. She was a very good Chair – a driver and wonderful at it, and Mabel remained as Vice-Chair until Suzy died. She did not want to take the Chair herself, but would help. Mr Emrys Roberts then became Chairman and before it closed, Miss Janet Morris, who had been Secretary, took over the Chair. She was of farming stock and had connections with Llangwyfan.

The Friends had sub-committees to deal with different aspects of their work. Mabel was on the Annual Fete Sub-Committee which raised money for equipment for the Hospital – beds, X-Rays etc. Her job was managing the teas, the entry ticket included a cup of tea and plated sandwich, scone and cake. Queues would quickly form in the Dining Hall when tea was served and people would scan the plates to find the best looking one before picking one up. A team of wives from the locality would work all morning preparing the teas and putting them together, with everyone enjoying themselves and having great fun. If anything ran out during the afternoon, it was a catastrophe. Mabel acted as waitress, clearing the tables for the next lot to sit down.

The kitchen used was behind the Dining Hall stage as the main kitchen was out of bounds for the event. The garden fete was held every year in June on the large lawn in front of the Administration Block. It had wonderful support from the community and there were numerous stalls, the cake stall being very popular.

The Committee would meet once a month. The Treasurer was a Bank Manager, and a Solicitor, Ivor Watkins, would offer advice if there were legal issues. Mabel's first husband died in 1979 and she moved to live in Brynrhyd yr Arian and worked in HM Stanley Hospital as a Tutor teaching Student Nurses obstetrics and parentcraft.

The League of Friends Committee were called to help during an influenza epidemic in the late 1960's for nursing patients in Llangwyfan and she offered her services for this. Whenever there was a shortage of staff the League of Friends could offer help, bringing patients and relatives to Hospital if transport was difficult.

Miss Janet Morris

I have mentioned above that Miss Janet Morris had Llangwyfan connections. In Fig 1 it is shown that her grandmother Janet was the second daughter of Moses and Jane Roberts (Fig 1).

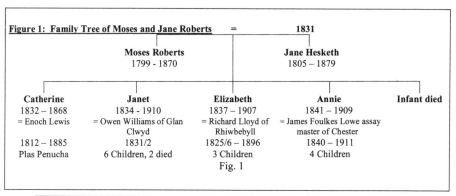

Figure 1: Family Tree of Moses and Jane Roberts = 1831

Moses Roberts		Jane Hesketh
1799 - 1870		1805 – 1879

Catherine	Janet	Elizabeth	Annie	Infant died
1832 – 1868	1834 - 1910	1837 – 1907	1841 – 1909	
= Enoch Lewis	= Owen Williams of Glan	= Richard Lloyd of	= James Foulkes Lowe assay	
	Clwyd	Rhiwbebyll	master of Chester	
1812 – 1885	1831/2	1825/6 – 1896	1840 – 1911	
Plas Penucha	6 Children, 2 died	3 Children	4 Children	
		Fig. 1		

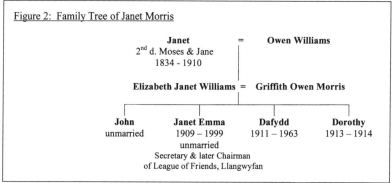

Figure 2: Family Tree of Janet Morris

Janet = Owen Williams
2nd d. Moses & Jane
1834 - 1910

Elizabeth Janet Williams = Griffith Owen Morris

John	Janet Emma	Dafydd	Dorothy
unmarried	1909 – 1999	1911 – 1963	1913 – 1914
	unmarried		
	Secretary & later Chairman		
	of League of Friends, Llangwyfan		

Janet [1834-1910] married Owen Williams of Carreg y Penill, Llanrhaeadr, moving to live in Glanclwyd, Bodfari. They had six children, two of whom died young. When Janet Roberts was 15 years old she kept a small tooled leather bound Welsh Notebook dated 8th July 1849 on the subject of sermons (Testunae Pregethau) and Chapel matters. This continued the family's strong religious convictions.

The first entry was on the 3rd June 1849. In 1850, 1852 and 1855 there were mentioned monthly Chapel meetings (Cyfarfod Misol). In 1870 there is a list of names with money on the side, which I presume was the collection given to the Chapel. There is no heading but I expect it was in shillings and pence:-

Edward Hesketh, Carreg y Penill, Llanrhaeadr 1-0
Catherine Hesketh   1-0
Catherine Williams   6
Janet Roberts   5-0
Jane Jones   1-6
John Evans   3-0
Thomas Williams   2-6
William Jones   2-6

It seems that Janet gave the most at 5-0 and the total is 17 shillings. Towards the end of the book, hymns were written out:-

• O fryniau Caersalem ceir gweled
• Cyfarchion ar wyl priodas.

Owen and Janet Williams had a daughter Elizabeth Janet Williams who married Griffith Owen Morris and their daughter Janet was a most efficient and industrious Secretary and later Chairman of the Llangwyfan League of Friends (Fig. 2).

Mrs Claudia Davies

Mrs Claudia Davies, wife of Dr Ifor Davies of Cerrigydrudion was a founder member of Llangwyfan League of Friends along with Mrs Suzy Hughes and she later became Chairman of the League.
  An appeal was launched in July 1956 by the people at Uwchaled to raise a fund to purchase a piano for Llangwyfan.

171

This followed the last meeting of the local committee of the Llanrwst National Eisteddfod in 1951 when a surplus of £39 remained and it was agreed that this be handed over to form the nucleus of a local fund to purchase a piano for the recreation of the patients and staff. £145 was raised and a piano purchased from Rushworth and Draper in 1957. As there was money left in the fund goldfish for the pond and rose bushes for the gardens were also purchased and presented.

MORE MEMORIES OF LLANGWYFAN
– J GWYN HUGHES

1. WARTIME

In addition to the male and female nurses on Block Six there was a colourful domestic named Agnes but affectionately known as Aggie. Her main duties were cleaning and washing and sterilising crockery in the kitchen. She also helped to carry the meals to the patients ending with "Ave you all 'ad". This was followed by a roar from the patients "Yes Aggie we've all 'ad".

In the photograph in volume one titled Birthday Party the celebration was for the little boy in the bed who came from Rhyl. His obituary appeared in the Daily Post in 2008. He would have been in his seventies. Also in the picture is Sister Frances ("Spanner") Roberts. Peering from just behind Sister Roberts is a patient remembered only by the nickname RAWKIS. This puzzled me until I discovered that Sister Roberts had once complained about his raucous singing! He used to wander around the grounds singing the only two songs in his repertoire:

"Telephone to Glory
Oh Joy divine
I feel the current flowing
down the line."

Then

"I'm in love with the girl I left behind me
more, more, more than ever before
Left right, left right mile after mile
I'm rehearsing for that march down the aisle."

Then

"Telephone to Glory ...."

Which provoked cries from the wards "For pity's sake sing something else if it's only "God Save The King." The musical tastes of the patients were largely confined to songs heard on the radio. A popular Western of the time was called "I've got too much Texas in my Bones" which the denizens of Block Six sang as "I've got too much TB in my Bones" to the consternation of their visitors.

As Block Six was an orthopaedic block there were, inevitably, a number of amputees who had sometimes lost a complete leg or otherwise an ankle. There were some six of them during my time there and they went for walks together on old-fashioned wooden crutches. Their progress was slow and stately and as they appeared around a corner they reminded me of a fleet of Spanish galleons sailing towards their meeting with Drake (or the more formidable Dr Hawkins).

Apart from the orthopaedic and gland cases there were two patients suffering from the deadly TB Meningitis and neither survived. The disfiguring disease Lupus also afflicted a few female patients in the nearby Block Five and two members of the domestic staff, a male porter and a female domestic had been scarred for life.

Block Six had no Day Room in which patients could relax and this was a considerable drawback since all one could do in wet weather was to hang around in the wards. Realising this Dr Hawkins discovered a disused store room on the ground floor and had some chairs and tables installed. He made a fine speech at its official opening and urged patrons to borrow books from the hospital library and to bring them back to read in the new recreation room. Returning two hours later, Dr Hawkins could barely see across the room for a thick cloud of cigarette smoke. The recreation room was promptly closed and never reopened.

The staff had a recreation room at the top of the hill near the Lights Department where occasional whist drives and dancing to records were held. On one occasion my friend Hugh Williams and I were invited to a social evening there, the outstanding memory of which is a retirement presentation to a lady from the dining room staff. One of her duties had been to prepare coffee and sandwiches for the Doctors and visiting surgeons and she was proud of her independence in this post. In her acceptance speech she astonished her audience by declaring "In all the years I knew Dr Hawkins – he never interfered with me".

2. RETURN TO LLANGWYFAN

After his retirement from the police, my father worked at Llangwyfan as Assistant in the Path Lab. As I had a few months gap between completing a project in Liverpool and taking up an appointment in London, he suggested that I should join him for the summer and I was warmly welcomed as a temporary ward orderly in company with John Lloyd, the Matron's nephew, her niece from South Africa and several school-leavers: we were referred to collectively as "the holiday makers".

We worked in The Huts as the wards of the wartime military wing were now styled. Llangwyfan was now a general hospital as TB had been mainly conquered in this country, but there were still a number of orthopaedic cases while a number of beds were occupied by cancer patients. The Huts boasted a fair sprinkling of eccentrics including a Polish ex-soldier whose corner bed in Hut D gave him a clear view of the graveyard of St Cwyfan's Church opposite. Every night this patient enraged his companions by calling to the occupants of the graveyard "Good night friends; soon I come to join you: wait for me please."

A young man had a speech impediment which made it difficult to understand his requirements. It was sometime before I realised that "I won a Yectic Yazor in a Yaffle" meant that he had won an electric razor in a raffle. Some of his bored friends started feeding him large numbers of pooled boiled eggs, in the hope of gaining an entry in The Guinness Book of Records, but Charge Nurse D R Jones discovered the plan before any real harm was done.

What time does Dr Penrhyn Jones go to bed?

On occasion I would be on late duty in Hut D, usually in the company of John Lloyd and a Nurse. At about 8.30 pm a phone call would come from the Deputy Medical Officer, Dr Penrhyn Jones, whose house was nearby, asking us to switch off our refrigerator as it was affecting his television. We did not like to leave it off too long so about 11.00 pm one of us would go outside the doctor's house to see if his family had retired for the night. No lights on downstairs would suggest that they had all gone to bed and the 'fridge would be switched on again.

Dr Penrhyn Jones was a fine doctor and a literate Welshman. On one occasion I had helped to bring a patient to the X-ray department for a somewhat complicated procedure. Dr Jones wanted the patient to lie half turned on his side. Having difficulty in getting the patient to understand what was required he eventually said in Welsh "Fel mae nw yn eistedd yn yr Set Fawr." ("As they sit in the Chapel Deacons' seats"). The man got the idea straight away and half turned on the table to gaze in a superior manner at his imaginary congregation.

My own attempts at utilising the Welsh language were less successful. Dr Gallagher was interviewing a new patient who spoke little English. "Ask him if he is able to go to the toilet by himself or whether his relatives have to help him". Thinking of the colloquial Welsh for toilet I referred to "Y ty bach" (the little house) whereupon the patient gave a cry of alarm and made to climb out of bed. "In heaven's name what have you said to the poor man?" cried Dr Gallagher. A patient in a nearby bed explained that my jumbled phrase had asked him if he knew that his relatives were selling his little house!

The face in the mirror

Strolling down from the huts to the dining hall I was intrigued by the sight of a disembodied face peering at me from a window in Block Seven. This turned out to be that of a girl who had been imprisoned in a plaster bed for many months and for whom the hospital carpenter had made a mirror on a pedestal so that she could see something of the outside world. It became the practice for people going up or down the main pathway to pause and wave at her which cheered her no end. Once or twice some of us would call to see her and, as a lover of Llandudno, I greatly envied Joan Vaughan her address – the lighthouse on the Great Orme, where her father was the Keeper.

Arriving at the dining hall one entered a haven of strict protocol. Diners sat at long tables according to a strict order of precedence. The Sisters and Charge Nurses sat at the first table nearest the entrance. At the next table sat the Staff Nurses and then the third table was for the Student Nurses. The last table was for Orderlies and State Enrolled Auxiliary Nurses.

At the end of the meal no one budged until the Sisters had all left together and then those at the other tables filed out in turn in the proper order of precedence. The Doctors and senior staff ate elsewhere and were darkly suspected of consuming superior meals in more luxurious surroundings.

On Fridays the dining hall assumed the role of wages office, as staff were called from the wards in groups to receive their pay. I had a shock on my first visit being told that the first week's remuneration would be kept in hand until I eventually left the hospital employment. This was to discourage people from doing a 'flit and leaving without notice'. As people left the hall feverishly tearing open their pay envelopes they would forget the eager hands waiting in the corridor – the Union Shop Steward collecting his dues and an Assistant Matron issuing national savings stamps. One could decline the latter but then ran the risk of being assigned a lengthy period of night duty.

Salaries in the National Health Service were not over-generous and many members of staff resorted to 'moonlighting' to augment their income. One Staff Nurse invested in a small printing machine and had quite a thriving business supplying Christmas cards to local villages and farms. The Matron, taking a party of friends to dine at a hostelry near Caerwys, was astonished to find one of her night duty staff serving behind the bar and two of her Nurses waitressing!

Llangwyfan's reputation attracted Doctors and Nurses from many different countries. Among them was Staff Nurse Anne Frome who came from Germany to improve her English. On the advice of a friend she bought The Times newspaper and studied every page when off duty. After six months she spoke the best English and knew more about world affairs than anyone else in the hospital! Some years later I ran into her in Waterloo Station. She was now working as a Midwife in Portsmouth and was extremely busy – "These Sailors think of nothing else".

Previous volumes have recorded the fine work done in the children's ward and Block Eight, like all the others, had its share of characters. One of them was a five year old boy named Barry who had a badly distorted spine and whose prognosis was very poor. On one occasion my father was chatting with Dr Gallagher outside the Lights Department when Barry approached them. My father pointed at a large conifer tree nearby and asked Barry if he knew that there were fairies in the tree. The little boy scornfully rubbished the idea and my father told him to close his eyes whilst he called "Fairies please send Barry some sweets". He then threw some sweets into the branches from where they fell onto the head of an astonished Barry who shouted to Dr Gallagher "The buggers have heard him".

CHAPTER 10

MISCELLANEOUS

- **Dismissal of Staff**. Throughout the books there are instances of dismissal of staff – in Gwyn Hughes and Anwen Jones' memories. On the 3rd September 1950 I read that a male student nurse was dismissed because he walked off the ward in the middle of his duty without any explanation to his Senior Officers.
- Sister Holden, a Night Superintendent in the early 1950's had a self-contained flat on the top floor of Cwyfan, where it was quiet.
- **TB Badges**. One gross of badges to an approved design was agreed to be purchased by the Finance Sub-Committee of Clwyd and Deeside HMC in June 1950, at a cost of 12 shillings and two pence each, and the cost defrayed from the "Free Monies" account. These were to be presented to the Nursing Staff who qualified for the Tuberculosis Association Certificate.
- Due to the remoteness of the North Wales Sanatorium from the centre of the population, and the large number of nursing staff employed, this resulted in additional administrative work in reimbursing the cost of the journeys made by the nursing staff to the nearest centre of the population. An application was made to the Ministry of Health for the authority to pay the sum of 16 shillings monthly to each member of nursing staff in order to cover the cost per week of one journey to Denbigh and one to Rhyl.

April 1950 (Finance Sub-Committee)

- In 1950 the HMC approved the suggestion of employing Italian Doctors to study in Llangwyfan (this was before Dr Biagi was employed).
- In 1950 it was reported that five pigs had died in transit.
- In 1964 German Nurses were recruited for Llangwyfan, with a considerable number who stayed and married local people – Ann Frohme and "Rudi" being remembered.
- A letter from Dr Biagi to Dr Penrhyn Jones in 1962 points out that in 1913-14 Dr Paterson tried to get male patients only in Llangwyfan so that they could contribute as graders, to do extra uncompleted work which needed to be done, such as drainage and terracing. However, he had to accept female patients who he agreed could work as hard as men.
- A Scot set up the Physiotherapy Department in the top huts. He was followed by Mr Day who committed suicide.
- The uniform of the nursing staff was lovely, it commanded respect and confidence to the patient that the wearer knew what they were doing. *(One of several remarks on these lines)*.
- Karen Messham and her partner now rent the garages and old Mortuary in 2008. The Mortuary slab of white porcelain was still there and concreted in, but has since been taken out.
- **Vernon Kellett Jones, Dental Surgeon at Llangwyfan [1951 -1980], died on the 7th May 2008.** His eldest grandson, Michael, in his tribute to him described a quiet family man. I remember him as a very kind gentleman with whom I had an excellent professional relationship at his Dental Surgery in Ruthin. His late wife, Margaret Coop, was a Radiographer in Llangwyfan and has also been mentioned earlier.
- The top entrance of Llangwyfan was just before the Deputy Medical Superintendent's home which was the new Plas Llangwyfan. Next to it was a Joiners Workshop and then garages which were used for maintenance of the Lister Trucks. The shop was behind the Dining Room and is in a very dilapidated state in 2008.

- The School for the children is the building to the side of X-ray on one side and Hut C on the other. The long building above it was known to Peter Wilson as Hut E and housed Occupational Therapy, the Pulmonary Laboratory and a Storeroom before becoming a Recreational Hall and a Plaster Room. The student nurse training school was in the old Light Department, along with the Dental Room, Pathology Laboratory, Dispensary and a Recreation Room. The pond was in the trees below Blocks 8 and 9. Peter Wilson had a room in the Top Bungalow in the 1960's – then called the Day Bungalow.
- The Laundry was near the Power House with the Sewing Room above.
- There was a small Air Raid Shelter below Block 3 and to the side of the Administration Block. Peter Wilson kept his motorbike – registered number plate FUN 597 there when he was resident. The Shelter has gone (2008).
- Bungalows: In 1957 the Top Bungalow (1) was called the Day Bungalow for Ancillary Staff and housed over 20 small rooms. In 1923 this was the Nurses Home.
- The next two were a semi-detached pair of bungalows: (1) for Assistant Matron, Miss Coombs, and the (2) for overnight staff. This was Tan Rhiw (this has now been demolished (2008). The next bungalow (3) was semi-detached:
  Bungalow (1) called Hafan was for Matron
  Bungalow (2) was for Junior Medical Staff.
- Nurses going back to their quarters in the Bungalow would at certain times of year come across what seemed like hundreds of Toads walking across the path from the pond to the lake above Llangwyfan. The squeamish would scream bringing the boilerman out to see what was happening.
- Mrs Edith Dickens gave an account of the Big Snowfall of 1965 in the Village Voice, Llandyrnog, January 2007, Vol 11, Issue 9. She was living at Tŷ'n Llan Farm at the time and remembers the difficulties she experienced of getting to the hospital with

walls of snow almost to the top of the houses on the road going up to the hospital; meeting up with others trying to get there, crossing fields with difficulty and eventually conquering the mountain of snow to be met by Matron Morris and several doctors who cheered their arrival. Although several people managed to walk home that night Matron Morris insisted that she stayed and slept in her bungalow. Jack Jones, the Hospital Chauffeur managed to drive a van down to the Police Station where all the food for the hospital had been left.

ABBREVIATIONS

HMD	Hugh Morriston Davies
WNMA	Welsh National Memorial Association
BTA	British Tuberculosis Association Certificate
WRHB	Welsh Regional Hospital Board
CHA	Clwyd Health Authority
C&D HMC	Clwyd and Deeside Hospital Management Committee
FRO	Flintshire Record Office
RRO	Ruthin Record Office
CO	Conscientious Objector
MMR	Mass Miniature Radiology
AP	Artificial Pneumothorax
PP	Pneumoperitoneum
INAH	Isoniazid
PAS	Para-amino Salicylic Acid
CPN	Community Psychiatric Nurse
MS	Medical Superintendent
PTS	Preliminary Training School
SRN	State Registered Nurse
SEN	State Enrolled Nurse
TSC	Theatre Services Centre
CSSD	Central Sterile Supplies Department
YGC	Ysbyty Glan Clwyd
SSAFA	Soldiers, Sailors and Airmen's Families Association
GP	General Practitioner
RSCN	Registered Sick Children's Nurse

BIBLIOGRAPHY

Chapter 1
Reference:
Tannahill M M & Higson P J – The use of behavioural interventions in changing the symptomatic behaviours of people who have chronic schizophrenia (research project of North Wales Hospital, Denbigh), page 4.

Oral Testimony: Peter Wilson

Chapter 6
Dr Tim Alban Lloyd
Ref: Obituary (CHJ) 1983 BMJ. Vol: 286
Family & Newspaper Testimony

Chapter 8.1
Ref: Prif Weinidog Answyddogol Cymru. y Lolfa. 2007
Jenkins G

CORRECTIONS AND ADDITIONS

LLANGWYFAN – SANATORIUM TO HOSPITAL

Second group photographs

- 16th page – Names of all in this group provided by Sr Norma Waine and photograph re-published.
- 17th page – Fancy Dress Party 1960s – Children. Names provided by Sr Norma Waine.
- 19th page – The Porters. Title change to Male Ancillary Staff. Goronwy Morris (Porter) standing behind *left to right:* Emrys Roberts (Orderly), Bob Roberts (Orderly), Myrddin Roberts (Orderly), Emlyn Davies (Porter)
- 25th page – Staff Group 1960s. Back row: Dr Streedharan, Dr Havinder Sahota, Dr T K Gandhi SHO, Block 9.
- 26th page – Miss Morris' Retirement. Greta Jones is between Sr Allerton and Ch/N Glyn Jones. ? on left.
- 31st page – Gardeners 1964. Mr Edwards (Farm Bailiff), Thomas Henry Evans (Head Gardener), Wilf Davies (Stores Porter), Horace Priest (Hospital Engineer).

Third group of photographs

- 9th page – Nurse Olwen Hughes with Sister Bassett, Outpatient Sister.
- 12th page – Incorrect photograph of Dr Hawkins. Correct photograph in *Llangwyfan Magic, Vol 1 – Lest We Forget.*

LLANGWYFAN MAGIC, VOLUME 1

- Page 41, 3rd paragraph, penultimate line: ... after 30 minutes "or" should go before "by boiling".